B

BALI TRAVEL

GUIDE 2023

The Complete Guide To Planning Your Trip To Bali, Including What To Do, Where To Stay, How To Stay Safe, And Many Amazing Attractions.

Natalie R. Pate

Welcome To Bali

Emily had always dreamed of visiting Bali. She had heard stories of its beautiful beaches, lush jungles, and vibrant culture, and she couldn't wait to see it all for herself. So, when she finally landed at Denpasar International Airport, she felt like she was on top of the world.

As soon as she stepped off the plane, Emily was struck by the warm, humid air and the tropical scent of the island. She made her way through the airport and found her driver, who was waiting to take her to her hotel. The drive was a bit chaotic, with motorcycles and scooters zooming past her window and vendors selling everything from fresh fruit to handmade crafts on the street corners. But Emily didn't mind. She was too excited to be in Bali to let a little bit of traffic get her down.

When she arrived at her hotel, she was greeted by the friendly staff and immediately felt at home. Her room was beautiful, with a balcony overlooking the ocean and a private outdoor shower. Emily decided to take a quick nap before heading out to explore the island.

After a few hours of rest, Emily was refreshed and ready to see Bali. She started her day by visiting the famous Tanah Lot Temple, a Hindu temple perched on a rocky outcropping in the sea. As she walked around the temple, she marveled at the intricate carvings and the stunning views of the ocean. She also took in the local culture, watching as the Balinese people made offerings to the temple and participated in traditional dances.

Next, Emily decided to take a hike through the lush jungles of Ubud. As she walked along the winding paths, she saw monkeys swinging from the trees and heard the chirping of exotic birds. She also visited a traditional Balinese village, where she saw the locals going about their daily lives and learned about the island's ancient customs.

After a day of exploring, Emily was ready to relax on the beach. She went to Kuta, one of Bali's most popular beaches, and spent the afternoon lounging on the sand, swimming in the crystal-clear waters, and watching the sun set over the ocean.

The next day, Emily decided to take a cooking class to learn more about Balinese cuisine. She had always loved cooking, and she couldn't wait to try her hand at making traditional dishes like Nasi Goreng (Indonesian Fried Rice) and Satay (marinated meats grilled on skewers). The class was a great success, and Emily learned how to make all sorts of delicious dishes that she would later replicate for her family and friends back home.

On her last day in Bali, Emily took a tour of the island's famous rice terraces. She rode a bike through the picturesque fields and learned about the traditional farming methods used by the Balinese. She also visited a local market where she picked up some souvenirs to take back home.

As Emily prepared to leave Bali, she felt a tinge of sadness. She had had the trip of a lifetime, and she knew she would miss the island's beauty, culture, and people. But she also knew that she would be back, as this trip had opened her eyes to all the beauty and wonder of the world, and she couldn't wait to explore more of it.

CHAPTER 1: INTRODUCTION

Beyond its natural beauty and rich culture, Bali is also known for its holistic wellness offerings. The island is home to a variety of yoga retreats, spas, and healing centers that offer everything from yoga classes and massages to traditional Balinese healing ceremonies. Visitors can indulge in a variety of treatments and therapies that focus on physical, emotional, and spiritual well-being.

Bali is also a shopper's paradise, with a wide range of traditional and modern markets, boutiques, and shopping centers. Visitors can find anything from handmade crafts, batik fabrics, and silver jewelry to designer clothing and luxury goods. The island is also home to a thriving fashion and design scene, with many local designers and brands creating unique and fashionable items.

In addition to its many attractions, Bali is also known for its friendly and welcoming people. The locals are known for their hospitality, and many visitors find themselves struck by the warmth and kindness of the Balinese. Visitors can immerse themselves in the local culture and experience the traditional way of life by staying in a local homestay or participating in a village tour.

Overview Of Bali

Bali is an Indonesian island located in the westernmost end of the Lesser Sunda Islands, lying between Java to the west and Lombok to the east. It is one of the country's 33 provinces with the provincial capital at Denpasar towards the south of the island. Bali is the home of the country's largest Hindu population and also the largest tourist destination in the world, with a yearly average of 4.3 million visitors. The island's history is marked by a series of powerful empires, each of which left their mark on the island's culture and architecture.

One of the main attractions in Bali is its beautiful beaches. The island is home to some of the most famous and beautiful beaches in the world, such as Kuta, Seminyak, and Nusa Dua. These beaches offer a wide range of activities for visitors, from swimming and sunbathing to surfing and diving. The island's beaches are also known for their beautiful sunsets, which are a popular attraction among visitors.

Another major attraction in Bali is its ancient temples and traditional villages. The island has a rich history of Hindu and Buddhist influence, which is reflected in its many temples and traditional villages. Visitors can explore ancient temples such as Pura Tanah Lot, Pura Besakih, and Uluwatu Temple, and experience traditional ceremonies and festivals. In addition, visitors can also explore traditional villages such as Ubud and Penestanan, where they can witness the daily life of the island's inhabitants and learn about the island's ancient customs and traditions.

Bali is also known for its lush jungles and beautiful rice terraces. The island's interior is covered in dense jungles, home to a variety of exotic animals and plants. Visitors can take a hike through the jungles and explore waterfalls, hot springs, and ancient temples hidden deep in the jungle. The island's rice terraces, located in Ubud and Jatiluwih, are also a popular attraction for visitors. These terraces are a testament to the island's agricultural heritage and offer stunning views of the surrounding landscape.

Bali is also famous for its delicious food. The island's cuisine is a mix of traditional Balinese and Indonesian dishes, with a strong influence from Chinese, Indian, and Dutch cuisine. Visitors can try traditional dishes such as Nasi Goreng, Satay, and Babi Guling, as well as seafood dishes such as Ikan Bakar and Mie Goreng. The island is also home to a wide range of local and international restaurants, where visitors can try a variety of cuisines.

The island is also well known for its wellness offerings. Bali is home to a wide range of yoga retreats, spas, and healing centers that offer everything from yoga classes and massages to traditional Balinese healing ceremonies. Visitors can indulge in a variety of treatments and therapies that focus on physical, emotional, and spiritual well-being. In addition, Bali is also home to many healing centers that offer Ayurvedic and Naturopathic treatments.

Finally, Bali is a shopper's paradise, with a wide range of traditional and modern markets, boutiques, and shopping centers. Visitors can find anything from handmade crafts, batik fabrics, and silver jewelry to designer clothing and luxury goods. The island is also home to a thriving fashion and design scene, with many local designers and brands creating unique and fashionable items.

Weather And Climate In Bali

Bali has a tropical climate, which means that it is hot and humid throughout the year, with temperatures averaging around 27-33 degrees Celsius (81-91 degrees Fahrenheit). The island has two main seasons: the dry season, which runs from April to September, and the wet season, which runs from October to March. During the dry season, Bali experiences less rainfall, which is the best time for tourists to visit, as it is mostly sunny and the sky is clear blue. While during the wet season, Bali experiences heavy rainfall, making it less suitable for outdoor activities.

The dry season is the best time to visit Bali if you are looking for clear, sunny weather and a chance to enjoy the island's many beaches. During this time, the humidity is relatively low, and the temperatures are mild and comfortable, making it the perfect weather for outdoor activities such as swimming, sunbathing, and exploring the island. The dry season is also the peak tourist season in Bali, with the majority of visitors coming to the island between June and September.

The wet season is less popular among tourists, but it can still be a good time to visit Bali if you are looking for a more authentic experience. During this time, the island experiences heavy rainfall, and the weather can be quite unpredictable. However, the wet season is also the time when the island's rice fields are at their greenest, and the many waterfalls and rivers are at their fullest. It can be a great time to explore the island's many temples and cultural sites, as well as to experience the traditional Balinese way of life.

Even during the wet season, rainfall tends to be concentrated in the late afternoon and evening, leaving the mornings and early afternoons mostly sunny. So, you can still make plans for activities like a sightseeing tour, a day spa, or even heading out to the beaches, but it's always a good idea to keep an eye on the weather forecast and be prepared for sudden rain showers.

Throughout the year, Bali experiences relatively high humidity, which can make the heat feel more intense. To avoid heat exhaustion, it is important to stay hydrated and to protect yourself from the sun. Sunscreen and a wide-brimmed hat are essential, and it is also a good idea to wear lightweight, breathable clothing.

Bali is also prone to occasional natural hazards such as volcanic eruptions, earthquakes, and tsunamis. But the overall risk is low, and the government has made significant efforts to reduce the potential impact of these hazards on the population and the tourism industry.

Best Time To Visit Bali

The dry season, which runs from April to October, is considered the best time to visit Bali for those looking to enjoy the island's beaches and outdoor activities. During this time, the weather is generally sunny and warm, with little chance of rain. The sea is also calm, making it perfect for swimming, surfing, and diving. Additionally, the dry season is also the peak tourist season, so expect higher prices and more crowded beaches.

The wet season, which runs from November to March, is considered the best time to visit Bali for those looking for a more laid-back and quieter experience. During this time, the island receives the most rainfall, but it is still possible to enjoy the island's many attractions. The monsoon season in Bali is less humid, making it more comfortable to explore the island. Prices are also lower during this time, and the beaches are less crowded, so it's a good time to visit Bali if you want to avoid the crowds. The wet season is also the best time to see the beautiful rice terraces, as the fields will be lush and green.

Another factor to consider when planning your trip to Bali is the local festivals and ceremonies. Bali is home to many traditional ceremonies and festivals, such as the Nyepi Day of Silence and the Galungan and Kuningan ceremonies. These events can make it difficult to find accommodation and transportation, so it is best to plan your trip around these events.

The best time to visit Bali depends on your personal preferences and what you want to do during your trip. The dry season, from April to October, is the best time to visit Bali for those looking to enjoy the island's beaches and outdoor activities, while the wet season, from November to March, is best for those looking for a more laid-back and quieter experience. It's also essential to plan your trip around the local festivals and ceremonies to avoid any inconvenience. Bali is a beautiful island with endless things to see and do, so no matter when you decide to visit, you're sure to have an unforgettable experience.

Getting To Bali

Getting to Bali, the "Island of the Gods," is relatively easy thanks to its well-connected international airport. Denpasar International Airport, also known as Ngurah Rai International Airport, is the main airport serving Bali and is located in the southern part of the island. It is one of the busiest airports in Indonesia and serves as a hub for many airlines. Visitors can fly to Bali from many major cities around the world, making it a convenient destination for travelers.

One of the most popular ways to get to Bali is by flying. There are many international airlines that operate flights to Bali, including

Air Asia, Garuda Indonesia, Qantas, and Singapore Airlines. The flight from major cities such as Sydney, Melbourne, and Singapore takes around 3-4 hours, while flights from major cities in Europe and the United States take around 12-15 hours. Visitors can also fly to Bali from major cities in Indonesia, such as Jakarta, Surabaya, and Lombok, with flights taking around 1-2 hours.

Another way to get to Bali is by taking a cruise. Many cruise lines, such as Celebrity Cruises, Royal Caribbean, and Princess Cruises, offer itineraries that include Bali as a port of call. Visitors can take a cruise from major cities in Asia, Australia, and the United States, and enjoy the scenic views of the ocean while they make their way to Bali.

It's also possible to get to Bali by land, but it's not the most popular way as it's quite a long trip. Visitors can take a train or bus from major cities in Java, such as Surabaya and Yogyakarta, and make their way to Bali. However, the journey can take up to 12 hours, and the quality of the trains and buses can vary, so it's best to book your tickets in advance and prepare for a long journey.

Visitors can also take a ferry from the neighboring island of Lombok, which takes around 2-3 hours. The ferry service is a convenient and relatively affordable way to get to Bali, especially if you're traveling from Lombok, but the service can be affected by weather conditions and sea conditions.

Once you have arrived in Bali, visitors can get around the island using various modes of transportation. Taxis and private cars are the most convenient way to get around the island, but they can be expensive. Visitors can also take a motorbike or car rental to get around the island, but it's essential to have an international driving license. Visitors can also take a bus or train to get around the island, but the services are limited, and it can be difficult to get to some destinations.

Visa Requirements

Tourist Visa-Free:

Many countries are eligible for a tourist visa-free entry to Bali for a stay of up to 30 days. This includes citizens from countries such as the United States, Canada, Australia, New Zealand, the United Kingdom, and many European countries. Visitors from these countries can enter Bali without a visa and stay for up to 30 days, but they must have a valid passport that is valid for at least six months.

Tourist Visa:

Citizens from some countries are eligible for a tourist visa, which allows them to stay in Bali for up to 60 days. This includes citizens from countries such as Russia, China, and India. Visitors from these countries must apply for a tourist visa before arriving in Bali and must have a valid passport that is valid for at least six months.

Business Visa:

Visitors who are traveling to Bali for business purposes must apply for a business visa. This visa allows visitors to stay in Bali for up to 60 days and can be extended for up to six months. Visitors must have a valid passport that is valid for at least six months, and they must have a letter of invitation from a local company or organization.

Work Visa:

Visitors who wish to work in Bali must apply for a work visa. This visa allows visitors to stay in Bali for up to 12 months and can be renewed. Visitors must have a valid passport that is valid for at least six months and must have a letter of invitation from a local company or organization.

It's important to note that visa requirements can change, and it's essential to check the most recent information before planning your trip. Visitors are also required to have a valid return or onward ticket and proof of sufficient funds for their stay in Bali.

Another important thing to note is that overstaying your visa can result in penalties, such as fines, or even being barred from entering Indonesia again. Visitors should ensure that they have the correct visa and make sure to extend it if they plan to stay longer than their initial visa allows.

It's also worth noting that the visa process may vary depending on the embassy or consulate you are applying through. Visitors should make sure to check with their local embassy or consulate to ensure they have the most up-to-date information and to gather all the required documents before they travel.

Additionally, it's always good to check with your travel insurance policy to see if it covers any visa or entry requirements, in case of any complications.

CHAPTER 2: TIPS FOR YOUR TRIP

Communication And Language

Communication and language are vital aspects of any society, and Bali is no exception. The island of Bali, located in Indonesia, has a unique linguistic and cultural landscape that reflects its history, influences, and its position as a major tourist destination.

The official language of Bali is Indonesian, which is a standardized form of Malay, spoken by the majority of the population. However, Balinese, a distinct Austronesian language, is also widely spoken on the island. Balinese is a complex language that uses many different levels of politeness, honorifics, and terms of address, which reflect the island's traditional social hierarchy.

In addition to Balinese and Indonesian, many Balinese people also speak a local dialect known as "Bali-krama" or "Bali-nguna", which is a colloquial version of the language. This dialect is used in informal settings and is considered to be a more relaxed and casual way of communicating.

Tourism has had a major impact on the language and communication of Bali. English is widely spoken by many

Balinese people, especially those working in the tourist industry, as it is the most common language spoken by visitors to the island. Many Balinese people also speak other languages such as Japanese and Chinese to cater to international tourists.

The Balinese are known for their friendliness and warmth, which is reflected in their communication style. Balinese people are typically very polite and indirect in their communication, and use nonverbal cues such as gestures and facial expressions to convey meaning. They also use a lot of indirect speech, such as hinting and implying, to avoid direct confrontation. This indirect communication style is thought to stem from the island's tradition of "gotong royong", which is a communal system of mutual help and cooperation.

Religion also plays a significant role in communication and language in Bali. Balinese Hinduism, which is the island's dominant religion, has a complex system of rituals and ceremonies, many of which involve the use of special languages and scripts. For example, the "Kawi" script is used to write religious texts and inscriptions, while "Sanskrit" and "Old Javanese" are used in religious ceremonies and rituals.

Money And Budgeting

Money and budgeting are important aspects of travel, and Bali, as a major tourist destination, offers a variety of options for managing your finances. It's essential to be aware of the local currency, exchange rates, and costs of goods and services to ensure that your trip to Bali is an enjoyable and affordable experience.

The currency used in Bali is the Indonesian Rupiah (IDR). The exchange rate varies, but as of January 2021, 1 USD is roughly equivalent to 14,000 IDR. It's important to note that many tourist-oriented businesses, especially in popular areas such as Kuta, Seminyak, and Ubud, will accept major foreign currencies, but the exchange rate may not be favorable. It's best to carry cash and use ATMs to withdraw Rupiah. Additionally, credit and debit cards are widely accepted in Bali, but it's a good idea to inform your bank of your travel plans before you depart to avoid any issues with blocked transactions.

Bali offers a wide range of accommodation options to suit all budgets. Budget travelers can find inexpensive guesthouses and hostels starting from around 75,000 IDR per night. Mid-range options, such as private rooms in homestays, can cost between 150,000 - 250,000 IDR per night. Luxury resorts and villas can cost upwards of 1,000,000 IDR per night. It's also worth noting that peak travel season, typically during school holidays, Christmas, and Easter, will result in higher prices for accommodation and flights.

Food is also a significant aspect of budgeting for a trip to Bali. Local warungs (small, family-owned restaurants) offer delicious and inexpensive meals, with prices starting around 15,000 IDR. Street food is also widely available and can be a cost-effective option for budget travelers. Mid-range restaurants, such as those found in tourist areas, can cost between 50,000 - 150,000 IDR for a meal. Fine dining establishments, particularly in five-star resorts, can be significantly more expensive.

Transportation costs in Bali are relatively low. Local buses, known as bemo, are widely available and very cheap, with fares starting at around 3,000 IDR. Taxis and private drivers are also an option, but it's important to agree on a price before starting the journey, as some drivers may take advantage of tourists. Renting a scooter is a popular and cost-effective option for getting around the island, with daily rentals starting at around 50,000 IDR.

One of the main draws of Bali is the island's many activities, such as surfing, yoga, and cultural tours. Prices for these activities can vary widely, with budget options, such as group surf lessons, starting at around 100,000 IDR, and luxury options, such as private surf lessons or spa treatments, costing significantly more.

Shopping is also a popular pastime in Bali, but it's important to be aware that prices can vary widely, particularly in tourist areas. Bargaining is expected and is an important part of the shopping experience, with discounts of up to 50% or more not uncommon. Additionally, be mindful of fake or low-quality products, which are commonly sold in tourist areas.

Etiquette And Customs

Etiquette and customs in Bali, an Indonesian island located in the westernmost end of the Lesser Sunda Islands, are an important aspect of Balinese culture. The island is known for its unique blend of Hindu and Buddhist influences, which are reflected in the customs and traditions of its people.

One of the most important customs in Bali is the practice of "tri hita karana," which translates to "three causes of well-being." This philosophy emphasizes the importance of maintaining a harmonious relationship with God, with other people, and with the environment. This concept is reflected in many aspects of Balinese life, including the way people dress, behave, and interact with each other.

When visiting Bali, it is important to dress modestly and cover your legs and shoulders. This is especially true when visiting temples, which are considered sacred spaces. Visitors should also be aware of the practice of "offering and prayer," which is an integral part of Balinese Hinduism. Offerings, which are made of a combination of flowers, rice, and other items, are placed in front of shrines and statues of gods and goddesses as a form of worship.

Another important aspect of Balinese culture is the practice of "bowing" as a sign of respect. Visitors should bow their heads slightly when greeting older or more senior people, or when entering or leaving a temple or other sacred space.

It's also important to note that Balinese people have a strong tradition of hospitality. So, if you are invited to someone's home, it is considered polite to bring a small gift, such as fruit or a traditional offering, as a sign of appreciation. It's also advisable to take off your shoes before entering someone's home as a sign of respect.

Tourism is a major industry in Bali, however it's still a traditional society where local customs and religious practices are deeply ingrained. Tourists should be mindful of and respectful of these customs. Nudity, for example, is not acceptable on the island. Balinese Hinduism prohibits public displays of affection as well. It's considered disrespectful to point your feet at a person or a religious object, so be mindful of your body language when you're sitting or standing.

In terms of food customs, it's customary to use the right hand when eating. The left hand is considered unclean, so be sure to only use your right hand to accept and eat food. It's also common to use your hands instead of utensils when eating traditional Balinese food.

Finally, it's important to be aware of the many ceremonies and festivals that take place in Bali throughout the year. These ceremonies are an important aspect of Balinese culture and are often accompanied by traditional dances and music. Visitors should be respectful of these events and not interfere or take photographs without permission.

CHAPTER 3: ACCOMMODATIONS

Luxury Hotels

The Mulia - This hotel located in Nusa Dua, known for its white sand beaches and crystal clear waters, The Mulia offers a range of luxurious villas and suites. All rooms are equipped with private balconies or terraces and offer stunning views of the ocean or garden. The hotel features a private beach, an infinity pool, and a spa, as well as a range of dining options and a fitness center. Prices start from $400 per night.

Alila Villas Uluwatu - This hotel is located on the cliffs of Uluwatu and offers a range of private pool villas with ocean views. Each villa features a private pool and outdoor shower, as well as a large private terrace. The hotel features a spa, a fitness center, a private beach club, and several dining options. Prices start from $450 per night.

The Chedi Club Tanah Gajah - This hotel is located in Ubud and offers a range of private pool villas, each featuring a private pool, outdoor shower and a terrace. The hotel features a spa, a fitness center, and several dining options. The hotel also offers guests the opportunity to participate in traditional cooking classes, and you can also take a stroll in the hotel's beautiful gardens. Prices start from $600 per night.

The Legian, Bali - This hotel is located in Seminyak, known for its luxurious shopping and dining scene. The hotel offers a range of private pool villas and suites, each featuring a private pool, outdoor shower, and terrace. The hotel features a spa, a fitness center, and several dining options. Prices start from $450 per night.

The Ayana Resort and Spa - This hotel is located in Jimbaran, known for its beautiful beaches and seafood restaurants. The hotel offers a range of private pool villas, each featuring a private pool, outdoor shower, and terrace. The hotel features a spa, a fitness center, and several dining options. The hotel also offers guests the opportunity to participate in traditional cooking classes and yoga sessions. Prices start from $450 per night.

The St. Regis Bali Resort - This hotel is located in Nusa Dua and offers a range of private pool villas and suites, each featuring a private pool, outdoor shower, and terrace. The hotel features a spa, a fitness center, and several dining options, including an all-day dining restaurant, a beachfront grill, and a steakhouse. Prices start from $600 per night.

Mid-Range Hotels

The Shanti Residence - This hotel is located in Sanur, known for its peaceful atmosphere and beautiful beaches. The hotel offers a range of comfortable rooms, each featuring a balcony or terrace. The hotel features a swimming pool, a spa, a fitness center, and several dining options. Prices start from $150 per night.

The Kayon Jungle Resort - This hotel is located in Ubud and surrounded by lush tropical gardens. The hotel offers a range of comfortable rooms, each featuring a balcony or terrace. The hotel features a swimming pool, a spa, a fitness center, and several dining options. Prices start from $200 per night.

The Tugu Bali - This hotel is located in Canggu, known for its surf culture and laid-back atmosphere. The hotel offers a range of comfortable rooms, each featuring a balcony or terrace. The hotel features a swimming pool, a spa, a fitness center, and several dining options. Prices start from $250 per night.

The Ubud Hanging Gardens - This hotel is located in Ubud and offers a range of comfortable rooms and private pool villas, each featuring a private pool, balcony or terrace. The hotel features a swimming pool, a spa, a fitness center, and several dining options. Prices start from $200 per night.

The Anantara Seminyak Bali Resort - This hotel is located in Seminyak, known for its luxurious shopping and dining scene. The hotel offers a range of comfortable rooms and private pool villas, each featuring a balcony or terrace. The hotel features a swimming pool, a spa, a fitness center, and several dining options. Prices start from $250 per night.

The Samaya Bali - This hotel is located in Seminyak and offers a range of comfortable rooms, each featuring a balcony or terrace. The hotel features a swimming pool, a spa, a fitness center, and several dining options. Prices start from $200 per night.

The Bisma Eight - This hotel is located in Ubud, known for its art, culture and beautiful scenery. The hotel offers a range of comfortable rooms, each featuring a balcony or terrace. The hotel features a swimming pool, a spa, a fitness center, and several dining options. The hotel also offers guests the opportunity to participate in traditional Balinese cooking classes and yoga sessions. Prices start from $150 per night.

The Padma Resort Ubud - This hotel is located in Ubud and offers a range of comfortable rooms, each featuring a balcony or terrace. The hotel features a swimming pool, a spa, a fitness center, and several dining options. The hotel also offers guests the opportunity to participate in traditional Balinese cooking classes, and you can also take a stroll in the hotel's beautiful gardens. Prices start from $200 per night.

The Royal Beach Seminyak Bali - This hotel is located in Seminyak, known for its luxurious shopping and dining scene. The hotel offers a range of comfortable rooms, each featuring a balcony or terrace. The hotel features a swimming pool, a spa, a fitness center, and several dining options, including an all-day dining restaurant, a beachfront grill, and a steakhouse. Prices start from $150 per night.

The Kamandalu Ubud - This hotel is located in Ubud and offers a range of comfortable rooms, each featuring a balcony or terrace. The hotel features a swimming pool, a spa, a fitness center, and several dining options. The hotel also offers guests the opportunity to participate in traditional Balinese cooking classes, and you can also take a stroll in the hotel's beautiful gardens. Prices start from $200 per night.

Budget Hotels

The Segara Village Hotel - This hotel is located in Sanur, known for its peaceful atmosphere and beautiful beaches. The hotel offers a range of basic rooms, each featuring a balcony or terrace. The hotel features a swimming pool, a spa, a fitness center, and several dining options. Prices start from $40 per night.

The Ubud Village Resort and Spa - This hotel is located in Ubud and offers a range of basic rooms, each featuring a balcony or terrace. The hotel features a swimming pool, a spa, a fitness center, and several dining options. Prices start from $60 per night.

The Anantara Seminyak Bali Resort - This hotel is located in Seminyak, known for its luxurious shopping and dining scene. The hotel offers a range of basic rooms, each featuring a balcony or terrace. The hotel features a swimming pool, a spa, a fitness center, and several dining options. Prices start from $80 per night.

The Kuta Seaview Boutique Resort & Spa - This hotel is located in Kuta, known for its vibrant nightlife and beautiful beaches. The hotel offers a range of basic rooms, each featuring a balcony or terrace. The hotel features a swimming pool, a spa, a fitness center, and several dining options. Prices start from $40 per night.

The Wina Holiday Villa Hotel & Spa - This hotel is located in Kuta and offers a range of basic rooms, each featuring a balcony or terrace. The hotel features a swimming pool, a spa, a fitness center, and several dining options. Prices start from $50 per night.

The Dewi Sri Hotel - This hotel is located in Legian, known for its vibrant nightlife and beautiful beaches. The hotel offers a range of basic rooms, each featuring a balcony or terrace. The hotel features a swimming pool, a spa, a fitness center, and several dining options. Prices start from $40 per night.

The Bali Fret Inn - This hotel is located in Kuta and offers a range of basic rooms, each featuring a balcony or terrace. The hotel features a swimming pool, a spa, a fitness center, and several dining options. Prices start from $25 per night.

The Puri Tirta Villas - This hotel is located in Ubud and offers a range of basic rooms and villas, each featuring a balcony or terrace. The hotel features a swimming pool, a spa, a fitness center, and several dining options. Prices start from $35 per night.

The Dwiki Guesthouse - This hotel is located in Ubud and offers a range of basic rooms, each featuring a balcony or terrace. The hotel features a swimming pool, a spa, a fitness center, and several dining options. Prices start from $20 per night.

The Balisani Padma Hotel - This hotel is located in Legian and offers a range of basic rooms, each featuring a balcony or terrace. The hotel features a swimming pool, a spa, a fitness center, and several dining options. Prices start from $30 per night.

Villas

The Mulia Villas - These villas are located in Nusa Dua, known for its white sand beaches and crystal clear waters. The villas offer a range of luxurious options, each featuring a private pool and outdoor shower, as well as a large private terrace. The villas feature a spa, a fitness center, and several dining options. Prices start from $600 per night.

Alila Villas Uluwatu - These villas are located on the cliffs of Uluwatu and offer a range of private pool villas with ocean views. Each villa features a private pool, outdoor shower, and a terrace. The villas feature a spa, a fitness center, a private beach club, and several dining options. Prices start from $800 per night.

The Chedi Club Tanah Gajah - These villas are located in Ubud and offer a range of private pool villas, each featuring a private pool, outdoor shower, and a terrace. The villas feature a spa, a fitness center, and several dining options. The villas also offer guests the opportunity to participate in traditional cooking classes, and you can also take a stroll in the hotel's beautiful gardens. Prices start from $1000 per night.

The Legian Private Villa - These villas are located in Seminyak, known for its luxurious shopping and dining scene. The villas offer a range of private pool villas, each featuring a private pool, outdoor shower, and terrace. The villas feature a spa, a fitness center, and several dining options. Prices start from $800 per night.

The Ayana Private Villa - These villas are located in Jimbaran, known for its beautiful beaches and seafood restaurants. The villas offer a range of private pool villas, each featuring a private pool, outdoor shower, and terrace. The villas feature a spa, a fitness center, and several dining options. The villas also offer guests the opportunity to participate in traditional cooking classes and yoga sessions. Prices start from $900 per night.

The St. Regis Bali Private Villa - These villas are located in Nusa Dua and offer a range of private pool villas, each featuring a private pool, outdoor shower, and terrace. The villas feature a spa, a fitness center, and several dining options, including an all-day dining restaurant, a beachfront grill, and a steakhouse. Prices start from $1000 per night.

The Samaja Villa - These villas are located in Seminyak, known for its luxurious shopping and dining scene. The villas offer a range of private pool villas, each featuring a private pool, outdoor shower, and terrace. The villas feature a spa, a fitness center, and several dining options. The villas also offer guests the opportunity to participate in traditional cooking classes and yoga sessions. Prices start from $800 per night.

The Villa Des Indes - These villas are located in Seminyak and offer a range of private pool villas, each featuring a private pool, outdoor shower, and terrace. The villas feature a spa, a fitness center, and several dining options. The villas also offer guests the opportunity to participate in traditional cooking classes and yoga sessions. Prices start from $1000 per night.

The The Villas at AYANA Resort - These villas are located in Jimbaran and offer a range of private pool villas, each featuring a private pool, outdoor shower, and terrace. The villas feature a spa, a fitness center, and several dining options. The villas also offer guests the opportunity to participate in traditional cooking classes and yoga sessions. Prices start from $1000 per night.

The The Royal Pita Maha - These villas are located in Ubud and offer a range of private pool villas, each featuring a private pool, outdoor shower, and terrace. The villas feature a spa, a fitness center, and several dining options. The villas also offer guests the opportunity to participate in traditional cooking classes and yoga sessions. Prices start from $900 per night.

Guesthouses

The Poppies Cottages - This guesthouse is located in Kuta, known for its vibrant nightlife and beautiful beaches. The guesthouse offers a range of basic rooms, each featuring a balcony or terrace. The guesthouse features a swimming pool, a spa, a fitness center, and several dining options. Prices start from $15 per night.

The D'Omah Guesthouse - This guesthouse is located in Ubud and offers a range of basic rooms, each featuring a balcony or terrace. The guesthouse is known for its traditional architecture, and it's surrounded by lush green gardens. Guests can take a stroll in the hotel's beautiful gardens and enjoy the serene atmosphere of Ubud. Prices start from $20 per night.

The Pertiwi Guesthouse - This guesthouse is also located in Ubud and offers a range of basic rooms, each featuring a balcony or terrace. The guesthouse is known for its traditional architecture, and it's surrounded by lush green gardens. The guesthouse features a swimming pool, a spa, a fitness center, and several dining options. Prices start from $15 per night.

The Ramayana Guesthouse - This guesthouse is located in Kuta and offers a range of basic rooms, each featuring a balcony or terrace. The guesthouse features a swimming pool, a spa, a fitness center, and several dining options. It is within walking distance to the beach and the famous Kuta nightlife. Prices start from $20 per night.

The Hatten House - This guesthouse is located in Sanur, known for its peaceful atmosphere and beautiful beaches. The guesthouse offers a range of basic rooms, each featuring a balcony or terrace. The guesthouse features a swimming pool, a spa, a fitness center, and several dining options. Prices start from $10 per night.

The Putri Bali Guesthouse - This guesthouse is located in the heart of Seminyak, known for its luxurious shopping and dining scene. The guesthouse offers a range of basic rooms, each featuring a balcony or terrace. The guesthouse features a swimming pool, a spa, a fitness center, and several dining options. Prices start from $20 per night.

The Dewi Sri Guesthouse - This guesthouse is located in Legian, known for its vibrant nightlife and beautiful beaches. The guest house offers a range of basic rooms, each featuring a balcony or terrace. The guesthouse features a swimming pool, a spa, a fitness center, and several dining options. Prices start from $15 per night.

The Bali Rani Guesthouse - This guesthouse is located in Nusa Dua, known for its white sand beaches and crystal clear waters. The guesthouse offers a range of basic rooms, each featuring a balcony or terrace. The guesthouse features a swimming pool, a spa, a fitness center, and several dining options. Prices start from $20 per night.

The Bali Bidadari Guesthouse - This guesthouse is located in Uluwatu, known for its beautiful cliffs and scenic views. The guesthouse offers a range of basic rooms, each featuring a balcony or terrace. The guesthouse features a swimming pool, a spa, a fitness center, and several dining options. Prices start from $20 per night.

The Bali Oka Guesthouse - This guesthouse is located in Lovina, known for its black-sand beaches and dolphin watching. The guesthouse offers a range of basic rooms, each featuring a balcony or terrace. The guesthouse features a swimming pool, a spa, a fitness center, and several dining options. Prices start from $15 per night.

Hostels

The Simple Hostel - This hostel is located in Kuta, known for its vibrant nightlife and beautiful beaches. The hostel offers a range of dormitory-style rooms, as well as private rooms with shared bathrooms. The hostel features a swimming pool, a common area, a restaurant and bar. Prices start from $5 per night for dormitory style room and $10 for private room.

The Bunk Bali - This hostel is located in Legian and offers a range of dormitory-style rooms, as well as private rooms with shared bathrooms. The hostel features a swimming pool, a common area, a restaurant and bar, and a rooftop terrace. Prices start from $6 per night for dormitory style room and $12 for private room.

The Bali Backpackers Hostel - This hostel is located in Ubud, known for its traditional culture and beautiful landscapes. The hostel offers a range of dormitory-style rooms, as well as private rooms with shared bathrooms. The hostel features a swimming pool, a common area, a restaurant and bar, and a yoga studio. Prices start from $5 per night for dormitory style room and $10 for private room.

The Kuta Beach Club Hostel - This hostel is located in Kuta, known for its vibrant nightlife and beautiful beaches. The hostel offers a range of dormitory-style rooms, as well as private rooms with shared bathrooms. The hostel features a swimming pool, a common area, a restaurant and bar, and a rooftop terrace. Prices start from $5 per night for dormitory style room and $10 for private room.

The The Lost Hostel - This hostel is located in Canggu, known for its beautiful beaches and surf culture. The hostel offers a range of dormitory-style rooms, as well as private rooms with shared bathrooms. The hostel features a swimming pool, a common area, a restaurant and bar, and a surf school. Prices start from $6 per night for dormitory style room and $12 for private room.

The Green Room Hostel - This hostel is located in Seminyak, known for its luxurious shopping and dining scene. The hostel offers a range of dormitory-style rooms, as well as private rooms with shared bathrooms. The hostel features a swimming pool, a common area, a restaurant and bar, and a rooftop terrace. Prices start from $6 per night for dormitory style room and $12 for private room.

The Bali Bliss Hostel - This hostel is located in Uluwatu, known for its beautiful cliffs and scenic views. The hostel offers a range of dormitory-style rooms, as well as private rooms with shared bathrooms. The hostel features a swimming pool, a common area, a restaurant and bar, and a yoga studio. Prices start from $6 per night for dormitory style room and $12 for private room.

The Bali Buddha Hostel - This hostel is located in Ubud, known for its traditional culture and beautiful landscapes. The hostel offers a range of dormitory-style rooms, as well as private rooms with shared bathrooms. The hostel features a swimming pool, a common area, a restaurant and bar, and yoga classes. Prices start from $5 per night for dormitory style room and $10 for private room.

The Bali Green Light Hostel - This hostel is located in Nusa Dua, known for its white sand beaches and crystal clear waters. The hostel offers a range of dormitory-style rooms, as well as private rooms with shared bathrooms. The hostel features a swimming pool, a common area, a restaurant and bar, and a rooftop terrace. Prices start from $6 per night for dormitory style room and $12 for private room.

CHAPTER 4: TRANSPORTATION (GETTING AROUND BALI)

Taxis And Ride-Sharing Services

Taxis are a popular form of transportation in Bali, and can be found in most tourist areas and major towns. Prices for taxi rides in Bali are generally regulated, and consumers can expect to pay a fair price for their ride. Taxis in Bali are generally metered, and prices depend on the distance traveled. For example, a ride from the airport to a popular tourist destination such as Kuta or Seminyak would cost around IDR 100,000-150,000 (approximately $7-10). However, prices can vary depending on the location, time of day and traffic. You should also note that some taxi drivers may try to charge tourists a higher price than locals, so it's important to know the standard prices and negotiate the price with the driver before starting the trip.

Ride-sharing services like Grab and Go-Jek have become increasingly popular in Bali in recent years. These services offer a convenient way to get around using a smartphone app. Prices for ride-sharing services in Bali are generally cheaper than taxis, and consumers can see the price of their ride before requesting it. For example, a ride from the airport to Kuta or Seminyak would cost around IDR 60,000-80,000 (approximately $4-5) using Grab or

Go-Jek. However, prices can vary depending on the location, time of day, and demand. Like in other places, during peak hours or bad weather, prices might increase, it's called surge pricing.

It's worth noting that both taxis and ride-sharing services in Bali can be affected by traffic, which can make travel times unpredictable. During peak hours or in areas with heavy traffic, rides may take longer and cost more.

When it comes to expenses, another important thing to consider is the cost of the app and data usage. To use ride-sharing apps like Grab and Go-Jek, you will need to download them on your smartphone, which is free. However, you should keep in mind that these apps use a lot of data, so it's best to use them when connected to Wi-Fi. If you don't have Wi-Fi, it's worth checking your data plan to make sure it includes enough data to cover the usage of the app. If not, you may incur extra charges for data overages.

Motorbikes And Scooters

One of the biggest advantages of renting a motorbike or scooter in Bali is the cost. Motorbike and scooter rentals in Bali are relatively cheap, with prices typically ranging from IDR 50,000-150,000 (approximately $3.5-10) per day. Some rental companies may offer discounts for long-term rentals or multiple days. Additionally, fuel is also relatively cheap in Bali, making it an affordable option for getting around the island.

Riding a motorbike or scooter in Bali can also be a great way to explore the island's many hidden gems, as it allows you to reach remote areas that might be difficult to access by car or public transportation. Additionally, it's possible to navigate narrow roads and small villages, something that might not be possible by car.

However, it's important to note that riding a motorbike or scooter in Bali can be dangerous, especially for those who are not experienced riders. Bali's roads can be unpredictable, with a mix of well-paved roads and poorly-maintained roads, and traffic can be heavy in some areas. Additionally, driving conditions can be challenging, with poor visibility and sudden stops or turns. It's essential to wear a helmet and obey traffic laws while riding, and to be aware of the potential hazards of the road.

Before renting a motorbike or scooter, it's important to make sure that the vehicle is in good condition and properly maintained. You should also ask about the rental company's policy for damages, as you may be held liable for any damages incurred while the vehicle is in your possession. Additionally, you should always carry your driver's license and your passport, as this may be required by the rental company.

In Bali, you can find different types of motorbikes and scooters, from the smallest one that's suitable for city traffic, to larger ones that are better suited for long distance and off-road travel. Prices will vary accordingly, and it's important to consider your needs, the type of trip you are planning, and your level of experience when choosing a vehicle.

When it comes to expenses, it's also worth noting that rental companies may require a deposit, which is typically refundable upon return of the vehicle. Make sure to ask about the deposit policy before renting and have a clear agreement on that.

Renting a motorbike or scooter in Bali can be a great way to see the island at your own pace, and it can be an affordable option for getting around. However, it's important to consider the potential dangers of riding on the island's roads and to be prepared for the unpredictable driving conditions. By taking proper precautions and choosing a suitable vehicle, tourists can safely enjoy the freedom and flexibility of exploring Bali on two wheels.

Bicycles

Bicycles are a popular form of transportation in Bali, offering a more environmentally friendly and leisurely way to explore the island. Bicycling allows tourists to experience the local culture, and see the beautiful landscapes at a slower pace while also being good for the environment and for your health. In this article, we will discuss the costs and benefits of renting a bicycle in Bali, as well as safety tips for riding on the island.

One of the biggest advantages of renting a bicycle in Bali is the cost. Bicycle rentals in Bali are relatively cheap, with prices typically ranging from IDR 20,000-50,000 (approximately $1.5-3.5) per day. Some rental companies may offer discounts for long-term rentals or multiple days. Additionally, since bicycles don't need fuel, it's an even more affordable option for getting around the island.

Riding a bicycle in Bali can also be a great way to explore the island's many hidden gems, as it allows you to reach remote areas that might be difficult to access by car or motorbike. Additionally, it's possible to navigate narrow roads and small villages, something that might not be possible by car or motorbike.

However, it's important to note that riding a bicycle in Bali can be dangerous, especially for those who are not experienced riders. Bali's roads can be unpredictable, with a mix of well-paved roads and poorly-maintained roads, and traffic can be heavy in some areas. Additionally, driving conditions can be challenging, with poor visibility and sudden stops or turns. It's essential to wear a helmet and obey traffic laws while riding, and to be aware of the potential hazards of the road.

Before renting a bicycle, it's important to make sure that the bicycle is in good condition and properly maintained. You should also ask about the rental company's policy for damages, as you may be held liable for any damages incurred while the bicycle is in your possession. Additionally, you should always carry your passport, as this may be required by the rental company.

In Bali, you can find different types of bicycles, from simple beach cruisers to multi-geared bicycles. Prices will vary accordingly, and it's important to consider your needs, the type of trip you are planning, and your level of experience when choosing a bicycle.

When it comes to expenses, it's also worth noting that rental companies may require a deposit, which is typically refundable upon return of the bicycle. Make sure to ask about the deposit policy before renting and have a clear agreement on that.

Public Transportation

Buses are one of the most affordable and convenient forms of public transportation in Bali. They run regularly and cover most areas of the island, making them a great option for budget-conscious travelers. Buses come in different types, the traditional bemo (microbus) and modern air-conditioned buses. Prices vary depending on the distance, but on average, a bus ride in Bali will cost around $0.20 - $1.

Taxis are another popular form of transportation in Bali. They can be hailed on the street or booked in advance through a variety of apps and websites. Most taxi companies in Bali use metered fares, which are calculated based on the distance and duration of the ride. However, some drivers may try to negotiate a flat rate for a journey, particularly for longer trips. On average, a taxi ride in Bali will cost around $3- $4 for the first 3 km, and $0.5 for each additional km.

Ride-hailing services such as Grab, Go-Jek and Bluebird are also available in Bali and have become increasingly popular in recent years. These services allow you to book a ride through a smartphone app, and they typically offer a range of vehicle options, including cars, motorbikes, and even bicycles. They also provide an estimate of the fare for the journey before you book, making it easy to compare prices with other transportation options. A ride-hailing service ride in Bali can cost around $3 - $8 depending on the distance.

Motorbike rentals are a popular option for tourists in Bali, as they offer a more flexible and convenient way to explore the island. Many companies offer motorbike rentals, and the prices vary depending on the type of motorbike and the length of the rental period. On average, a motorbike rental in Bali will cost around $5 - $10 per day, but prices can be negotiated for a longer rental period.

Car rentals are also available in Bali, but they tend to be more expensive than motorbike rentals. Prices vary depending on the type of car and the length of the rental period. On average, a car rental in Bali will cost around $30 - $50 per day, and they can be booked through various rental companies or online platforms.

When it comes to public transportation in Bali, buses and taxis are considered to be the most affordable options, but ride-hailing services, motorbike rentals, and car rentals are also readily available. it's always a good idea to compare prices and check for deals and discounts before making a final decision on which mode of transportation to use.

It's worth noting that during peak season, prices for transportation including rental may increase and availability may decrease, so it's important to plan in advance and book beforehand if possible. Additionally, it's essential to always check the condition of the vehicle before renting, whether it's a motorbike or a car, to ensure the safety of the trip.

Ferry Services

Ferry services are a popular and convenient way to travel between the different islands in Indonesia, and Bali is no exception. The island is well-connected by ferry services to other nearby islands, including Lombok, the Gili Islands, and the Nusa Islands. These services provide tourists and locals with an affordable and efficient way to explore the surrounding areas and discover the natural beauty of the region. In this article, we will discuss the various ferry services available in Bali, including their prices and schedules.

The most popular ferry service in Bali is the route from Padang Bai on the east coast of Bali to the three Gili Islands (Gili Trawangan, Gili Air, and Gili Meno) in Lombok. This route is operated by a number of different companies, and the ferries run regularly throughout the day. The journey takes around 2-3 hours, and the prices vary depending on the company and the class of service. On average, a one-way ticket on this route will cost around $15 - $30.

Another popular ferry service in Bali is the route from Sanur on the south coast of Bali to the island of Nusa Lembongan. This route is also operated by a number of different companies, and the ferries run regularly throughout the day. The journey takes around 30 minutes to 1 hour, and the prices vary depending on the company and the class of service. On average, a one-way ticket on this route will cost around $10 - $15.

There are also several other ferry services available in Bali that connect the island with other destinations in Indonesia, such as Java and Sumatra. These services run less frequently and typically take longer, but they can be a great way to explore the surrounding areas and discover the natural beauty of the region. Prices for these services vary depending on the route and the class of service, but they tend to be more expensive than the routes to the Gili Islands and Nusa Lembongan.

When it comes to ferry services in Bali, it's important to note that schedules and prices can vary depending on the season, and it's a good idea to check the most up-to-date information before planning your trip. Also, it's a good idea to book in advance if possible, as ferries can fill up quickly, especially during peak season.

In addition to scheduled ferry services, there are also a number of private charter services available in Bali, which offer more flexibility and convenience for travelers. These services typically include a speedboat or a traditional wooden boat and can take you to a variety of different islands and destinations. Prices for these services vary depending on the destination and the length of the trip, but they tend to be more expensive than scheduled ferry services.

It is also important to consider the safety regulations for the ferry services you intend to use. Ensure the company you are booking with have valid certifications and safety measures in place. Additionally, consider your personal safety, such as life jackets, emergency procedures and the overall condition of the vessel.

Ferry services in Bali offer an affordable and convenient way to explore the surrounding islands and discover the natural beauty of the region. There are a variety of services available, connecting Bali with destinations such as the Gili Islands, Nusa Lembongan, and other islands in Indonesia. Prices and schedules can vary depending on the route and the season, so it's always a good idea to check the most up-to-date information and book in advance if possible. Also, it is important to prioritize safety in your decision making process.

Car Rental

Car rental is a popular option for tourists and travelers visiting Bali, as it offers a more flexible and convenient way to explore the island. With car rental, you can easily navigate the island's winding roads and visit the many sights and attractions that Bali has to offer. Car rental companies are readily available throughout Bali, and they offer a wide range of vehicles to suit different needs and budgets. In this article, we will discuss the various car rental options available in Bali, including their prices and availability.

When it comes to car rental in Bali, there are several types of vehicles available to rent, including compact cars, sedans, SUVs, and vans. Compact cars and sedans are the most popular options among tourists and are suitable for navigating the island's winding roads and small streets. They are also the most affordable options, with prices starting at around $30 - $40 per day.

SUVs and vans are also available for rental in Bali, but they tend to be more expensive than compact cars and sedans. These vehicles are ideal for larger groups or families, as they offer more space and comfort. Prices for SUVs and vans start at around $50 - $60 per day.

When renting a car in Bali, it's important to note that rental companies often offer different rental packages, which can include various add-ons such as insurance and GPS navigation. Be sure to read the terms and conditions carefully to understand what is included in the rental price.

Most car rental companies in Bali require a valid international driver's license and a passport or ID card as identification. It's also important to note that traffic laws and regulations in Bali are different from those in many other countries, and it's important to familiarize yourself with them before driving on the island.

Additionally, car rental companies in Bali may require a deposit upon rental, which can be in the form of cash or a credit card hold.

It's also worth to check if the company offers 24-hour road assistance, as in case of unexpected events, such as breakdown or accidents, it's crucial to have a support.

There are also several online platforms and travel agencies that offer car rental services in Bali. These services allow you to easily compare prices and availability from different car rental companies and book your rental in advance. Some of the popular car rental platforms in Bali include rentalcars.com, bali.travel and balibestcarrental.com

When planning your trip, it's always a good idea to check for deals and discounts, as many car rental companies offer special rates for advance bookings or for longer rental periods. Additionally, as mentioned before, it's essential to always check the condition of the vehicle before renting, to ensure the safety of the trip.

CHAPTER 5: POPULAR TOURIST DESTINATION

Beaches

There are countless beaches to choose from in Bali, each with its own unique atmosphere and activities. In this article, we will take a closer look at some of the most popular beaches in Bali and examine the expenses associated with visiting them.

First on our list is Kuta Beach, located on the southern coast of Bali. This is one of the most popular and well-known beaches in Bali, and is known for its lively atmosphere and great surf. Visitors to Kuta Beach can enjoy a variety of activities such as swimming, sunbathing, and surfing. The beach is also surrounded by a variety of shops, restaurants, and bars, making it a great place to spend the day.

The cost of visiting Kuta Beach can vary depending on the time of year and the type of accommodation you choose. For example, staying in a budget hotel near the beach can cost as little as $20 per night, while staying in a luxury resort can cost upwards of $200 per night. The cost of food and drinks in the surrounding area can also vary, with a meal at a local warung (Indonesian food stall) costing around $5, while a meal at a more upscale restaurant can cost $20 or more.

Another popular beach in Bali is Seminyak Beach, located just north of Kuta. This beach is known for its white sand and clear blue waters, as well as its upscale restaurants and bars. Visitors to Seminyak Beach can enjoy a variety of activities such as swimming, sunbathing, and beach volleyball. The beach is also home to a number of luxury resorts and villas, making it a great place to relax and unwind.

The cost of visiting Seminyak Beach can also vary depending on the time of year and the type of accommodation you choose. For example, staying in a budget hotel near the beach can cost as little as $30 per night, while staying in a luxury resort can cost upwards of $300 per night. The cost of food and drinks in the surrounding area can also vary, with a meal at a local warung costing around $7, while a meal at a more upscale restaurant can cost $30 or more.

Next on our list is Nusa Dua Beach, located on the southern tip of Bali. This beach is known for its calm waters and white sand beaches, making it a great place for swimming and sunbathing. Visitors to Nusa Dua Beach can also enjoy a variety of water sports such as snorkeling, diving, and windsurfing. The beach is also surrounded by a number of luxury resorts and villas, making it a great place to relax and unwind.

The cost of visiting Nusa Dua Beach can also vary depending on the time of year and the type of accommodation you choose. For example, staying in a budget hotel near the beach can cost as little as $35 per night, while staying in a luxury resort can cost upwards of $350 per night. The cost of food and drinks in the surrounding area can also vary, with a meal at a local warung costing around $8, while a meal at a more upscale restaurant can cost $35 or more.

Finally, we come to Jimbaran Beach, located on the southern coast of Bali. This beach is known for its beautiful sunsets and its famous seafood restaurants. Visitors to Jimbaran Beach can enjoy a variety of activities such as swimming, sunbathing, and beach volleyball. The beach is also home to a number of luxury resorts and villas, making it a great place to relax and unwind The cost of visiting Jimbaran Beach can also vary depending on the time of year and the type of accommodation you choose.

For example, staying in a budget hotel near the beach can cost as little as $40 per night, while staying in a luxury resort can cost upwards of $400 per night. The cost of food and drinks in the surrounding area can also vary, with a meal at a local warung costing around $10, while a meal at a more upscale restaurant can cost $40 or more.

One of the most popular activities at Jimbaran Beach is dining at one of the seafood restaurants that line the beach. These restaurants serve a variety of fresh seafood dishes, such as grilled fish, shrimp, and squid, and are known for their affordable prices and delicious food. A meal at one of these restaurants can cost anywhere from $10 to $30 per person, depending on the type of seafood you order.

In addition to the expenses associated with visiting the beaches, there are also several other costs to consider when planning a trip to Bali. These include transportation costs, such as the cost of a taxi or rental car, as well as the cost of activities and excursions. For example, a day trip to a nearby island or a visit to a temple can cost anywhere from $20 to $50 per person.

Overall, the cost of visiting the beaches in Bali can vary depending on the time of year and the type of accommodation you choose. However, even if you choose to stay in a budget hotel and dine at local warungs, you can still enjoy a beautiful and memorable vacation on one of Bali's many beaches. It's important to keep in mind that a great deal of activities like watching sunset, dining in seafood restaurants and enjoying the ocean activities are free and won't cost you anything.

Surfing

First and foremost, the cost of renting a surfboard in Bali can vary depending on the location and the quality of the board. A basic surfboard can cost anywhere from $5 to $15 per day, while a high-performance board can cost $20 to $50 per day. For those who are just starting out or who want to take a lesson, many surf schools in Bali offer packages that include a board and lesson for around $30 to $50 per day.

In addition to the cost of renting a board, there are also several other expenses to consider when surfing in Bali. These include transportation costs, such as the cost of a taxi or rental car, as well as the cost of food and accommodation. For example, staying in a budget hotel near a surf spot can cost as little as $20 per night, while staying in a luxury resort can cost upwards of $200 per night. The cost of food and drinks can also vary, with a meal at a local warung (Indonesian food stall) costing around $5, while a meal at a more upscale restaurant can cost $20 or more.

Another important expense to consider is the cost of surf insurance. Many surf schools and rental shops in Bali require surfers to have insurance before they can rent a board or take a lesson. While the cost of insurance can vary, it typically ranges from $5 to $15 per day. It's important to have a surf insurance as it will cover the medical expenses if you have an accident while surfing.

If you're planning to spend a considerable amount of time surfing in Bali, it might be a good idea to invest in your own surfboard. The cost of buying a new surfboard can vary depending on the brand and the size, but it can be anywhere from $500 to $1000. Investing in your own surfboard will save you money in the long run as you won't have to rent one every time you want to surf.

Another expense to consider is the cost of a surf guide. Many surfers choose to hire a surf guide to help them find the best waves and avoid the crowds. The cost of a surf guide can vary depending on the length of the tour and the level of service provided, but it typically ranges from $50 to $100 per day.

Finally, it's worth mentioning that Bali has a wide range of surf spots, some of them are more crowded than others. Some spots are more suitable for beginners, while others are more challenging and suitable for experienced surfers. It's important to choose the right spot for your level and to avoid crowded places, as it will make your experience more enjoyable.

Temples And Cultural Sites

One of the most popular temples in Bali is the Uluwatu Temple, located on the southern tip of the island. This ancient Hindu temple is built on a cliff overlooking the Indian Ocean and is known for its stunning sunsets and breathtaking views. Visitors to Uluwatu Temple can also enjoy traditional Balinese dances, such as the kecak dance, which is performed at sunset.

The cost of visiting Uluwatu Temple can vary depending on the time of year and the type of tour you choose. For example, a basic tour that includes transportation to and from the temple and a guide can cost around $20 per person, while a more luxurious tour that includes a sunset dinner and traditional Balinese dance performance can cost upwards of $50 per person. Additionally, you'll be charged an entry fee to enter the temple, which is around $5 per person.

Another popular temple in Bali is the Tanah Lot Temple, located on the west coast of the island. This ancient Hindu temple is built on a rock formation in the middle of the sea and is known for its beautiful sunsets and stunning views. Visitors to Tanah Lot Temple can also enjoy traditional Balinese dances, such as the kecak dance, which is performed at sunset.

The cost of visiting Tanah Lot Temple can also vary depending on the time of year and the type of tour you choose. For example, a basic tour that includes transportation to and from the temple and a guide can cost around $25 per person, while a more luxurious tour that includes a sunset dinner and traditional Balinese dance performance can cost upwards of $60 per person. Additionally, you'll be charged an entry fee to enter the temple, which is around $5 per person.

Another important cultural site in Bali is the traditional Balinese village of Ubud. This charming village is known for its beautiful temples, traditional markets, and vibrant arts and crafts scene. Visitors to Ubud can explore the village's many temples, such as the Pura Taman Saraswati, and can also enjoy traditional Balinese dances, such as the kecak dance, which is performed at sunset.

The cost of visiting Ubud can vary depending on the type of accommodation you choose. For example, staying in a budget hotel in the village can cost as little as $20 per night, while staying in a luxury resort can cost upwards of $200 per night. Additionally, you'll be charged an entry fee to enter some of the temples and cultural sites, which can range from $3 to $5 per person.

In addition to the cost of visiting temples and cultural sites, there are also several other expenses to consider when planning a trip to Bali. These include transportation costs, such as the cost of a taxi or rental car, as well as the cost of food and drinks. For example, a meal at a local warung (Indonesian food stall) can cost around $5, while a meal at a more upscale restaurant can cost $20 or more.

Overall, the cost of visiting temples and cultural sites in Bali can vary depending on the time of year and the type of tour or accommodation you choose. However, even if you choose budget-friendly options, you can still enjoy a rich and memorable cultural experience in Bali. It's important to keep in mind that many of the temples and cultural sites in Bali are free to visit, and the entry fee is usually a small amount. Additionally, many of the temples and cultural sites offer traditional dance performances and ceremonies that are free to watch.

Another way to save money when visiting temples and cultural sites in Bali is to plan your trip during the low season, as prices tend to be lower during this time. Additionally, many temples and cultural sites offer discounts for students, children, and senior citizens, so it's worth checking if you qualify for any of these

Bali is a cultural paradise with a wealth of temples and cultural sites to explore. From the ancient Hindu temples of Uluwatu and Tanah Lot to the traditional Balinese villages of Ubud, there is something for everyone to enjoy. While the expenses of visiting these temples and cultural sites can vary, with a little bit of planning and budgeting, you can have a rich and memorable cultural experience in Bali without breaking the bank. It's important to consider all the expenses and plan accordingly to make the most of your cultural vacation in Bali.

Hiking And Outdoor Activities

One of the most popular outdoor activities in Bali is hiking in the Ubud region. The area is known for its lush jungles, beautiful rice terraces, and traditional villages. The most popular hiking trails in Ubud include the Campuhan Ridge Walk, the Tegalalang Rice Terrace Walk, and the Ubud Monkey Forest. Each of these trails offer a different experience, from breathtaking views to monkey-spotting.

The cost of hiking in Ubud can vary depending on the trail and the type of tour you choose. For example, a basic self-guided hike can cost as little as $5, while a guided tour with a local guide can cost upwards of $50. Additionally, you'll be charged an entry fee to enter some of the hiking trails, which can range from $2 to $5 per person.

Another popular outdoor activity in Bali is rock climbing and visiting the Uluwatu cliffs. The Uluwatu region is known for its rugged cliffs and beautiful beaches, making it a popular destination for rock climbers and adventure seekers. Visitors can climb the cliffs, take a guided tour and enjoy the stunning views of the Indian Ocean.

The cost of rock climbing in Uluwatu can vary depending on the type of tour or guide you choose. For example, a basic self-guided climb can cost as little as $20, while a guided tour with equipment rental can cost upwards of $50. It's important to note that the entry fee to climb some of the cliffs can range from $5 to $10 per person.

Another popular outdoor activity in Bali is white water rafting. The Ayung River in Ubud is the most popular location for rafting, offering exciting rapids and beautiful scenery. Visitors can take a guided rafting tour and enjoy the beautiful views of the river, passing through traditional villages and lush jungles.

The cost of white water rafting in Ubud can vary depending on the type of tour or guide you choose. For example, a basic self-guided rafting trip can cost as little as $20, while a guided tour with equipment rental can cost upwards of $50. It's important to note that the entry fee to raft some of the rivers can range from $5 to $10 per person.

In addition to the cost of these outdoor activities, there are also several other expenses to consider when planning a trip to Bali. These include transportation costs, such as the cost of a taxi or rental car, as well as the cost of food and accommodation. For example, staying in a budget hotel near a hiking trail or climbing spot can cost as little as $20 per night, while staying in a luxury resort can cost upwards of $200 per night. The cost of food and drinks can also vary, with a meal at a local warung (Indonesian food stall) costing around $5, while a meal at a more upscale restaurant can cost $20 or more.

Overall, the cost of hiking and outdoor activities in Bali can vary depending on the location and the type of tour or guide you choose. However, even if you choose budget-friendly options, you can still enjoy a beautiful and unforgettable outdoor experience in Bali. It's important to keep in mind that many of the outdoor activities in Bali are free to visit, and the entry fee is usually a small amount. Additionally, many of the outdoor activities offer discounts for students, children, and senior citizens, so it's worth checking if you qualify for any of these discounts.

CHAPTER 6: ADVENTURE AND ACTIVITIES

Water Sports

Surfing:

The cost of surfing in Bali varies depending on the location, equipment, and duration of the session. A one-hour surf lesson at a beginner-friendly spot such as Kuta can cost around $25, while a full-day surf trip to a more advanced spot such as Uluwatu can cost around $75. Renting a surfboard for a day can cost around $10-20.

Diving and Snorkeling:

The cost of diving and snorkeling in Bali varies depending on the location, equipment, and duration of the trip. A one-tank dive at a spot such as Menjangan Island can cost around $60-70, while a full-day snorkeling trip to Nusa Penida can cost around $50-60. Renting snorkeling equipment for a day can cost around $10-15.

Paddleboarding:

Paddleboarding is another popular water sport in Bali, with many spots offering calm waters and beautiful scenery. Some of the best places to paddleboard in Bali include the rice paddies in Ubud, the mangroves in Nusa Lembongan, and the temples in Tanah Lot.

The cost of paddleboarding in Bali varies depending on the location, equipment, and duration of the trip. Renting a paddleboard for a day can cost around $20-30, while a guided tour can cost around $50-60.

Other Water Sports:

Bali also offers a wide range of other water sports, including jet skiing, parasailing, and wakeboarding. The cost of these activities can vary depending on the location, equipment, and duration of the activity. A 15-minute jet ski ride can cost around $40-50, while a parasailing ride can cost around $50-70.

In conclusion, Bali offers a wide range of water sports for visitors to enjoy, from surfing and diving to paddleboarding and jet skiing. The costs associated with these activities can vary depending on the location, equipment, and duration of the activity, but generally, they are affordable and accessible to most visitors.

It's important to note that the costs mentioned in this article are approximate and can vary depending on the specific provider or location. It's also worth noting that many providers offer package deals that include multiple activities at a discounted rate. Additionally, it's always a good idea to shop around and compare prices before making a decision.

Another important factor to consider when planning a water sports trip to Bali is safety. Many providers in Bali are reputable and follow safety guidelines, but it's always a good idea to do your own research and make sure the provider you choose is reputable and has a good safety record. This is especially important when it comes to activities like diving and snorkeling, where safety guidelines must be strictly followed to ensure the safety of the participants.

In addition to the expenses, it's also important to consider the weather conditions in Bali, which can vary greatly depending on the time of year. The rainy season in Bali is between October to March, and during this time, some water sports may not be available due to rough seas and high winds. It's always a good idea to check the weather forecast before planning your trip and to be aware of any potential weather-related disruptions.

Bali is a great destination for water sports enthusiasts, offering a wide range of activities for visitors to enjoy. The associated expenses can vary, but are generally affordable and accessible to most visitors. Safety is a top priority and travelers should also consider the weather conditions before planning their trip. With a little bit of planning and research, you can have an unforgettable water sports experience in Bali.

Parasailing And Paragliding

Parasailing and paragliding are two popular aerial sports that offer a unique perspective of Bali's stunning landscape and beautiful beaches. Both activities involve gliding through the air while attached to a parachute or wing, and offer a thrilling experience for adventurers of all ages. In this article, we will take a closer look at parasailing and paragliding in Bali, including the costs associated with these activities.

Parasailing:

Parasailing in Bali involves being towed behind a boat while attached to a parachute. The activity allows participants to soar up to 300 feet in the air and enjoy panoramic views of the island's beaches, temples, and rice paddies. Some popular parasailing spots in Bali include Tanjung Benoa, Nusa Dua, and Kuta.

The cost of parasailing in Bali can vary depending on the location, duration of the ride, and type of package. A basic parasailing ride can cost around $50-70 for a single person, while a more advanced package can cost around $70-90 and includes multiple runs or a longer ride. It's also worth noting that many providers offer package deals that include multiple activities, such as jet skiing or banana boat rides, at a discounted rate.

Paragliding:

Paragliding in Bali involves using a powered paraglider to fly through the air. The activity allows participants to fly at a higher altitude than parasailing and offers a more intimate experience with the island's natural beauty. Some popular paragliding spots in Bali include Ubud, Lembongan, and Nusa Dua.

The cost of paragliding in Bali can vary depending on the location, duration of the flight, and type of package. A basic paragliding ride can cost around $70-90 for a single person, while a more advanced package can cost around $100-120 and includes a longer flight or multiple runs. It's also worth noting that many providers offer package deals that include multiple activities, such as tandem flights or video packages, at a discounted rate.

It's important to note that the costs mentioned in this article are approximate and can vary depending on the specific provider or location. It's also worth noting that many providers offer package deals that include multiple activities at a discounted rate. Additionally, it's always a good idea to shop around and compare prices before making a decision.

Another important factor to consider when planning a parasailing or paragliding trip to Bali is safety. Many providers in Bali are reputable and follow safety guidelines, but it's always a good idea to do your own research and make sure the provider you choose is reputable and has a good safety record. This is especially important when it comes to activities like parasailing and paragliding, where safety guidelines must be strictly followed to ensure the safety of the participants.

In addition to the expenses, it's also important to consider the weather conditions in Bali, which can vary greatly depending on the time of year. The rainy season in Bali is between October to March, and during this time, some water sports may not be available due to rough seas and high winds. It's always a good idea to check the weather forecast before planning your trip and to be aware of any potential weather-related disruptions.

Overall, Bali is a great destination for parasailing and paragliding enthusiasts, offering a wide range of activities for visitors to enjoy. The associated expenses can vary, but are generally affordable and accessible to most visitors. Safety is a top priority and travelers should also consider the weather conditions before planning their trip. With a little bit of planning and research, you can have an unforgettable parasailing and paragliding experience in Bali.

When considering parasailing or paragliding, it's also important to consider your own physical limitations and comfort level. Parasailing is generally considered to be a less strenuous activity and is suitable for a wider range of participants, while paragliding requires a bit more physical exertion and may not be suitable for everyone. It's always a good idea to speak with the provider in advance and discuss any concerns or limitations you may have.

Another important factor to consider is the level of experience you have with these activities. For first-time participants, it's recommended to opt for a shorter ride or a beginner-friendly package. For those with more experience, there are advanced packages available that offer longer rides or more challenging routes.

Both parasailing and paragliding are an incredible way to experience the natural beauty of Bali. Whether you're interested in taking in the sights from a new perspective or simply looking for a thrilling adventure, these activities offer something for everyone. With a little bit of planning and research, you can have an unforgettable parasailing and paragliding experience in Bali.

Rock Climbing And Rappelling

Rock Climbing:

Bali offers a variety of rock climbing opportunities for climbers of all skill levels. Some popular rock climbing spots in Bali include Ubud, Kintamani, and Uluwatu. These areas offer a range of routes, from beginner-friendly to advanced, and provide climbers with the opportunity to experience the island's beautiful landscapes from a unique perspective.

The cost of rock climbing in Bali can vary depending on the location, duration of the climb, and type of package. A basic rock climbing package can cost around $50-70 for a half-day climb and around $70-90 for a full-day climb. These packages typically include equipment rental and a guide. Advanced packages can cost around $100-120 and may include multiple climbs or more challenging routes. It's also worth noting that many providers offer package deals that include multiple activities, such as canyoning or abseiling, at a discounted rate.

Rappelling:

Rappelling in Bali involves descending steep cliffs or rock formations using a rope and harness. This activity is a popular option for those looking for a thrilling adventure and offers a unique perspective of the island's natural beauty. Some popular rappelling spots in Bali include Ubud, Kintamani, and Uluwatu.

The cost of rappelling in Bali can vary depending on the location, duration of the descent, and type of package. A basic rappelling package can cost around $50-70 for a half-day descent and around $70-90 for a full-day descent. These packages typically include equipment rental and a guide. Advanced packages can cost around $100-120 and may include multiple descents or more challenging routes. It's also worth noting that many providers offer package deals that include multiple activities, such as canyoning or rock climbing, at a discounted rate.

It's important to note that the costs mentioned in this article are approximate and can vary depending on the specific provider or location. It's also worth noting that many providers offer package deals that include multiple activities at a discounted rate. Additionally, it's always a good idea to shop around and compare prices before making a decision.

Another important factor to consider when planning a rock climbing or rappelling trip to Bali is safety. Many providers in Bali are reputable and follow safety guidelines, but it's always a good idea to do your own research and make sure the provider you choose is reputable and has a good safety record. This is especially important when it comes to activities like rock climbing and rappelling, where safety guidelines must be strictly followed to ensure the safety of the participants.

In addition to the expenses, it's also important to consider the weather conditions in Bali, which can vary greatly depending on the time of year. The rainy season in Bali is between October to March, and during this time, some water sports may not be available due to rough seas and high winds. It's always a good idea to check the weather forecast before planning your trip and to be aware of any potential weather-related disruptions.

Overall, Bali is a great destination for rock climbing and rappelling enthusiasts, offering a wide range of activities for visitors to enjoy.

The associated expenses can vary, but are generally affordable and accessible to most visitors. Safety is a top priority and travelers should also consider the weather conditions before planning their trip. With a little bit of planning and research, you can have an unforgettable rock climbing and rappelling experience in Bali.

When considering rock climbing or rappelling, it's also important to consider your own physical limitations and comfort level. Both activities can be physically demanding and require a certain level of fitness and stamina. It's always a good idea to speak with the provider in advance and discuss any concerns or limitations you may have.

Another important factor to consider is the level of experience you have with these activities. For first-time participants, it's recommended to opt for a shorter climb or descent or a beginner-friendly package. For those with more experience, there are advanced packages available that offer longer climbs or more challenging routes.

It's also worth noting that many providers offer guided tours which can be a great option for first-time participants as it provides an experienced guide who can ensure safety and provide instruction.

Bali's rocky cliffs and limestone formations provide a challenging and exhilarating experience for rock climbing and rappelling enthusiasts. With a variety of routes and locations to choose from, Bali offers something for climbers and rappellers of all skill levels. While these activities can be physically demanding, the breathtaking views and unique perspective of the island's natural beauty make it worth the effort. With a little bit of planning and research, you can have an unforgettable rock climbing and rappelling experience in Bali.

Zip-Lining And Canopy Tours

Zip-lining and canopy tours in Bali offer an exciting and unique way to experience the island's natural beauty. These activities involve soaring through the air while attached to a cable, and provide a thrilling perspective of Bali's lush jungles, waterfalls, and rice paddies. In this article, we will take a closer look at zip-lining and canopy tours in Bali, including the costs associated with these activities.

Zip-lining:

Zip-lining in Bali involves flying through the air while attached to a cable, typically suspended high above the ground. This activity is a popular option for those looking for a thrilling adventure and offers a unique perspective of the island's natural beauty. Some popular zip-lining spots in Bali include Ubud, Kintamani, and Uluwatu.

The cost of zip-lining in Bali can vary depending on the location, duration of the ride, and type of package. A basic zip-lining package can cost around $50-70 for a single ride or a half-day tour, while a full-day tour can cost around $70-90. These packages typically include equipment rental and a guide. Advanced packages can cost around $100-120 and may include multiple rides or more challenging routes. It's also worth noting that many providers offer package deals that include multiple activities, such as rock climbing or rappelling, at a discounted rate.

Canopy Tours:

Canopy tours in Bali involve walking or hiking through the jungle while connected to a series of platforms and zip-lines. This activity is a popular option for those looking to explore the island's natural beauty in a unique way. Some popular canopy tour spots in Bali include Ubud, Kintamani, and Uluwatu.

The cost of canopy tours in Bali can vary depending on the location, duration of the tour, and type of package. A basic canopy tour package can cost around $50-70 for a half-day tour, while a full-day tour can cost around $70-90. These packages typically include equipment rental, guides and transport to and from the location. Advanced packages can cost around $100-120 and may include additional activities such as rock climbing or rappelling. It's also worth noting that many providers offer package deals that include multiple activities at a discounted rate.

It's important to note that the costs mentioned in this article are approximate and can vary depending on the specific provider or location. It's also worth noting that many providers offer package deals that include multiple activities at a discounted rate. Additionally, it's always a good idea to shop around and compare prices before making a decision.

Another important factor to consider when planning a zip-lining or canopy tour trip to Bali is safety. Many providers in Bali are reputable and follow safety guidelines, but it's always a good idea to do your own research and make sure the provider you choose is reputable and has a good safety record. This is especially important when it comes to activities like zip-lining and canopy tours, where safety guidelines must be strictly followed to ensure the safety of the participants.

In addition to the expenses, it's also important to consider the weather conditions in Bali, which can vary greatly depending on the time of year. The rainy season in Bali is between October to March, and during this time, some water sports may not be available due to rough seas and high winds. It's always a good idea to check the weather forecast before planning your trip and to be aware of any potential weather-related disruptions.

Bali is a great destination for zip-lining and canopy tour enthusiasts, offering a wide range of activities for visitors to enjoy. The associated expenses can vary, but are generally affordable and accessible to most visitors. Safety is a top priority and travelers should also consider the weather conditions before planning their trip. With a little bit of planning and research, you can have an unforgettable zip-lining and canopy tour experience in Bali.

CHAPTER 7: WELLNESS AND RELAXATION

Yoga And Meditation

There are many different types of yoga and meditation retreats available in Bali, ranging from budget-friendly options to luxury retreats. Some popular styles of yoga offered in Bali include Hatha, Vinyasa, and Ashtanga yoga. Many retreats also offer a combination of yoga and meditation classes, as well as workshops on topics such as ayurveda and mindfulness.

The cost of a yoga and meditation retreat in Bali can vary greatly depending on the type of retreat and accommodations chosen. Budget-friendly options can start as low as $500 for a week-long retreat, while luxury retreats can cost upwards of $3000. The cost typically includes accommodations, meals, and yoga and meditation classes.

The accommodations at yoga retreats in Bali can range from basic shared rooms to luxurious private villas. Many retreat centers are located in secluded areas, surrounded by lush jungle and rice paddies, providing a peaceful and serene environment for yoga and meditation.

Meals at yoga retreats in Bali are typically vegetarian and made with locally sourced ingredients. Many retreats offer a mix of Indonesian and Western cuisine, and can accommodate special dietary needs.

In addition to yoga and meditation classes, many retreats also offer a variety of activities and excursions. These can include visits to temples, hiking in the jungle, and exploring local markets.

Bali is an excellent destination for those looking to deepen their yoga and meditation practice. With a wide variety of retreats to choose from, and a beautiful and spiritual environment, Bali offers something for everyone.

To sum up, Bali is a popular destination for yoga and meditation enthusiasts. There are many different types of yoga and meditation retreats available in Bali, ranging from budget-friendly options to luxury retreats. The cost of a yoga and meditation retreat in Bali can vary greatly depending on the type of retreat and accommodations chosen. Budget-friendly options can start as low as $500 for a week-long retreat, while luxury retreats can cost upwards of $3000. Accommodations at yoga retreats in Bali can range from basic shared rooms to luxurious private villas and meals are typically vegetarian and made with locally sourced ingredients. In addition to yoga and meditation classes, many retreats also offer a variety of activities and excursions.

Bali, an Indonesian island located in the westernmost end of the Lesser Sunda Islands, is a popular destination for yoga and meditation enthusiasts. The island is known for its beautiful beaches, lush jungles, and vibrant culture, making it the perfect place to reconnect with oneself and find inner peace.

There are many different types of yoga and meditation retreats available in Bali, ranging from budget-friendly options to luxury retreats. Some popular styles of yoga offered in Bali include Hatha, Vinyasa, and Ashtanga yoga. Many retreats also offer a combination of yoga and meditation classes, as well as workshops on topics such as ayurveda and mindfulness.

The cost of a yoga and meditation retreat in Bali can vary greatly depending on the type of retreat and accommodations chosen. Budget-friendly options can start as low as $500 for a week-long retreat, while luxury retreats can cost upwards of $3000. The cost typically includes accommodations, meals, and yoga and meditation classes.

The accommodations at yoga retreats in Bali can range from basic shared rooms to luxurious private villas. Many retreat centers are located in secluded areas, surrounded by lush jungle and rice paddies, providing a peaceful and serene environment for yoga and meditation.

Meals at yoga retreats in Bali are typically vegetarian and made with locally sourced ingredients. Many retreats offer a mix of Indonesian and Western cuisine, and can accommodate special dietary needs.

In addition to yoga and meditation classes, many retreats also offer a variety of activities and excursions. These can include visits to temples, hiking in the jungle, and exploring local markets.

Overall, Bali is an excellent destination for those looking to deepen their yoga and meditation practice. With a wide variety of retreats to choose from, and a beautiful and spiritual environment, Bali offers something for everyone.

To sum up, Bali is a popular destination for yoga and meditation enthusiasts. There are many different types of yoga and meditation retreats available in Bali, ranging from budget-friendly options to luxury retreats. The cost of a yoga and meditation retreat in Bali can vary greatly depending on the type of retreat and accommodations chosen. Budget-friendly options can start as low as $500 for a week-long retreat, while luxury retreats can cost upwards of $3000. Accommodations at yoga retreats in Bali can range from basic shared rooms to luxurious private villas and meals are typically vegetarian and made with locally sourced ingredients. In addition to yoga and meditation classes, many retreats also offer a variety of activities and excursions.

Spa And Massage

One of the most popular spa and massage treatments in Bali is the traditional Balinese massage. This massage is a blend of acupressure, reflexology, and gentle stretching, and is designed to improve circulation, release muscle tension and balance the body's energy. The massage is typically performed by two therapists, who work in synchrony to provide a deeply relaxing and rejuvenating experience. The cost of a traditional Balinese massage ranges from $20-$50 depending on the location and the length of the massage.

Another popular spa treatment in Bali is the traditional Indonesian Lulur, a full-body exfoliating treatment that uses a mixture of turmeric, sandalwood, and rice powder to remove dead skin cells and leave the skin soft and smooth. The treatment is usually followed by a massage with aromatic oils. The cost of a Lulur treatment ranges from $40-$80 depending on the location and the length of the treatment.

Bali is also home to a variety of modern spa treatments such as facials, body wraps, and hydrotherapy. These treatments are typically offered at luxury resorts and spas and can be quite expensive, with prices ranging from $80-$200. Some of these spas offer packages that include multiple treatments, such as a full-day spa package that includes a massage, facial, and body wrap.

Another option for spa and massage treatments in Bali is to visit a traditional Indonesian "jamu" spa. Jamu spas are traditional Indonesian healing centers that offer a variety of natural treatments such as herbal baths, scrubs, and massages. These spas often use locally sourced herbs and plants in their treatments, and the cost is typically lower than at modern spas, ranging from $20-$50.

Along with spa treatments, Bali is also known for its reflexology and traditional Chinese medicine centers. Reflexology is a form of massage that focuses on specific points on the feet, hands, and ears, and is said to promote healing and relaxation throughout the body. The cost of reflexology treatments ranges from $20-$40 per hour. Traditional Chinese medicine centers offer acupuncture and cupping therapy, which can help to alleviate pain, improve circulation and balance the body's energy. The cost of these treatments can range from $40-$80 per session.

Lastly, it's worth noting that Bali offers a variety of options for accommodation, from budget-friendly guesthouses to luxury resorts. Many resorts and hotels have spas on-site, offering a wide range of treatments, but also many standalone spas and massage centers can be found all over the island.

Bali offers a wide variety of options for spa and massage treatments. From traditional Balinese massages to modern spa treatments, there's something for everyone. The island's natural beauty, rich culture, and spiritual energy make it a perfect destination for those looking to relax and rejuvenate. With a range of options, there's something for everyone and all budgets. Whether you're looking for a traditional Balinese massage or a luxurious spa treatment, Bali has it all.

Health Retreats

Health retreats in Bali offer a variety of activities and services that are designed to promote physical, mental, and spiritual well-being. Some popular activities offered at health retreats include yoga and meditation, fitness classes, healthy cooking workshops, and outdoor activities such as hiking and surfing. Many retreats also offer workshops on topics such as nutrition, stress management, and personal development.

The cost of a health retreat in Bali can vary greatly depending on the type of retreat and accommodations chosen. Budget-friendly options can start as low as $500 for a week-long retreat, while luxury retreats can cost upwards of $3000. The cost typically includes accommodations, meals, and activities.

The accommodations at health retreats in Bali can range from basic shared rooms to luxurious private villas. Many retreat centers are located in secluded areas, surrounded by lush jungle and rice paddies, providing a peaceful and serene environment for the retreat.

Meals at health retreats in Bali are typically healthy, nutritious, and made with locally sourced ingredients. Many retreats offer a mix of Indonesian and Western cuisine, and can accommodate special dietary needs.

In addition to yoga and meditation classes, many retreats also offer a variety of activities and excursions. These can include visits to temples, hiking in the jungle, and exploring local markets.

Many health retreats in Bali also offer a variety of spa and wellness treatments such as massage, reflexology, and traditional healing therapies. These treatments can help to alleviate pain, improve circulation, and promote overall well-being. The cost of spa and wellness treatments can vary depending on the type of treatment and the length of the session, but generally ranges from $40-$100.

Another popular option for health retreats in Bali is taking private classes or workshops with local health and wellness experts. Many experienced health and wellness practitioners reside in Bali and offer private classes and workshops on a variety of topics such as nutrition, stress management, and personal development. These classes can be tailored to suit the individual's needs and can be held in a variety of settings such as in a studio, on the beach, or in the jungle. The cost of private classes can vary depending on the teacher and the length of the class, but generally ranges from $50-$100 per hour.

Lastly, it's worth noting that Bali offers a variety of options for accommodation, from budget-friendly guesthouses to luxury resorts. While staying in a health retreat center may offer more of a wellness-centric environment, many people choose to stay in a private accommodation or a hotel and take classes in a nearby studio. This allows for more flexibility and the ability to explore the island and its culture while still having access to health and wellness activities.

CHAPTER 8: FOOD AND DRINK

Traditional Balinese Cuisine

Traditional Balinese cuisine is a combination of various flavors and ingredients, primarily influenced by Hindu and Buddhist cultures. The island's rich and fertile soil, as well as the abundance of seafood from the surrounding waters, plays a significant role in the local cuisine. Balinese dishes are characterized by the use of a wide range of spices and herbs, such as turmeric, ginger, lemongrass, and chili, which give the food its unique flavor and aroma.

One of the most popular traditional dishes in Bali is "Bebek Bengil," which is crispy duck served with a variety of sauces and spices. The dish is traditionally cooked by marinating the duck in a mixture of spices and herbs, then deep-frying it until it becomes crispy and golden brown. Another popular dish is "Sate Lilit," which is minced seafood or meat mixed with spices and herbs, then wrapped around a bamboo skewer and grilled over charcoal.

Another traditional Balinese dish is "Lawar," which is a mixed vegetable dish made from grated coconut, mixed with meat or seafood, and flavored with a variety of spices and herbs. "Sate

Plecing" is another popular dish that originated from the island of Lombok, it is a type of sate (skewered meat) served with a spicy sauce made from chili, tomatoes, and shrimp paste.

Rice is a staple in Balinese cuisine, and it is typically served with most traditional dishes. "Nasi Campur" is a popular dish that consists of steamed rice served with a variety of side dishes such as meat, seafood, and vegetables. "Nasi Goreng" is another popular dish that is similar to fried rice but made with a unique blend of spices and seasonings.

For dessert, "Pisang Goreng" is a popular choice, which is deep-fried banana served with a sweet syrup or chocolate sauce. "Dadar Gulung" is another traditional dessert that is made from coconut milk, pandan leaves, and sugar, then rolled and served with grated coconut.

In terms of expenses, traditional Balinese cuisine is relatively affordable, with most dishes costing around $2 - $5 USD. Bebek Bengil, for example, typically costs around $5 - $8 USD, while a plate of Nasi Campur can be purchased for as little as $2 - $3 USD. Desserts are also relatively inexpensive, with most costing around $1 - $2 USD.

Overall, traditional Balinese cuisine is a delicious and unique blend of flavors and ingredients, influenced by the island's rich culture and history. With its affordable prices and wide variety of dishes, it is a must-try for anyone visiting Bali.

Seafood And International Dining

One of the highlights of Bali's culinary offerings is its seafood and international dining options. From fresh seafood caught daily by local fishermen to haute cuisine from around the world, Bali has something to offer for every palate.

Starting with seafood, Bali is home to an abundance of fresh seafood caught daily by local fishermen. The island's location in the middle of the Coral Triangle, which is known for its rich marine biodiversity, means that seafood is readily available and incredibly fresh.

One of the most popular seafood dishes in Bali is "Ikan Bakar," which is grilled fish served with a variety of sambals (spicy sauces) and spices. The fish is typically marinated in a mixture of turmeric, chili, and other spices before being grilled to perfection. Another popular dish is "Udang Goreng," which is fried prawns served with a spicy sambal.

For those looking for more upscale seafood dining options, Bali also offers a variety of high-end seafood restaurants. Some of the most popular include "Rock Bar" at Ayana Resort and Spa, which serves a variety of fresh seafood dishes while overlooking the Indian Ocean. "Sardine" is another popular seafood restaurant that offers a Mediterranean-inspired menu featuring a variety of seafood dishes.

In addition to seafood, Bali also offers a wide variety of international dining options. From Italian trattorias to French bistros, and even Japanese and Korean restaurants, Bali has something to offer for every taste.

One of the most popular international dining options in Bali is Italian cuisine. There are a variety of Italian restaurants on the island, serving everything from classic pasta dishes to wood-fired pizzas. "Da Maria" is a popular Italian restaurant that serves a variety of traditional Italian dishes in a chic and modern setting. "La Brisa" is another popular Italian restaurant that offers a beautiful ocean view and a menu featuring a variety of pasta dishes and wood-fired pizzas.

For those looking for Asian cuisine, Bali also offers a variety of Japanese and Korean restaurants. "Sardine" offers a Japanese-inspired menu featuring a variety of sushi and sashimi, while "Sari Organik" is a popular Korean restaurant that serves a variety of traditional Korean dishes in a beautiful setting surrounded by rice fields.

In terms of expenses, seafood and international dining in Bali can vary greatly. A plate of Ikan Bakar at a local warung (small restaurant) can cost around $2 - $3 USD, while a meal at a high-end seafood restaurant can cost upwards of $30 - $50 USD per person. Italian and Asian cuisine can also vary in price, with a meal at a casual trattoria or Korean restaurant costing around $10 - $15 USD per person, while a meal at a high-end restaurant can cost upwards of $50 - $70 USD per person.

Bali offers a diverse and delicious food scene, with something to offer for every palate. From fresh seafood caught daily by local fishermen to haute cuisine from around the world, Bali is a food lover's paradise. With a variety of dining options at different price ranges, it is easy to find a place that fits your budget and taste.

Local Markets And Street Food

Local markets, known as "pasar," and street food vendors, known as "warung," can be found all over the island, offering a variety of traditional Balinese dishes, seafood, and international cuisine.

One of the most popular local markets in Bali is the "Badung Market" in Denpasar, which is open daily from early morning until late evening. The market is a great place to find fresh produce, seafood, spices, and traditional Balinese clothing and souvenirs. Visitors can also find a variety of street food vendors at the market, serving everything from traditional dishes like "Nasi Goreng" (fried rice) and "Mie Goreng" (fried noodles) to seafood dishes like "Ikan Bakar" (grilled fish) and "Udang Goreng" (fried prawns).

Another popular local market is the "Kereneng Market" in Seminyak, which is known for its seafood vendors. Visitors can find a wide variety of fresh seafood, including fish, prawns, squid, and even octopus, that are caught daily by local fishermen. The seafood can be purchased and cooked on the spot by street food vendors, or taken to go.

For those looking for a more authentic street food experience, Bali also offers a variety of street food vendors, known as "warung," that can be found all over the island. These small, family-run restaurants offer a variety of traditional Balinese dishes at affordable prices. Some popular street food vendors include "Warung Made" in Ubud, which is known for its traditional Balinese dishes like "Lawar" (mixed vegetable dish) and "Sate Lilit" (minced seafood or meat skewers), and "Warung Tegal" in Seminyak, which is known for its seafood dishes like "Ikan Bakar" (grilled fish) and "Udang Goreng" (fried prawns).

In terms of expenses, local markets and street food in Bali are relatively affordable, with most dishes costing around $2 - $5 USD. A plate of Nasi Goreng at a local warung, for example, typically costs around $2 - $3 USD, while a plate of Ikan Bakar at a street food vendor can cost around $3 - $5 USD. Seafood can also be purchased at local markets at a reasonable price, with a pound of fresh prawns costing around $5 - $7 USD.

Bali offers a wide variety of local markets and street food options that are both delicious and affordable. Visitors can find a variety of traditional Balinese dishes, seafood, and international cuisine, all at a reasonable price. A visit to a local market or street food vendor is a great way to experience the local culture and taste the delicious food that Bali has to offer.

Coffee And Tea Plantations

Starting with coffee, Bali is home to a variety of coffee plantations, the most popular of which is the "Bali Pulina Coffee Plantation" located in the Gianyar Regency. The plantation is known for its Arabica coffee, which is grown on the slopes of Mount Agung, and provides a scenic view of the surrounding area. The plantation offers a variety of activities such as coffee tastings and tours of the plantation, where visitors can learn about the process of growing and harvesting coffee.

Another popular coffee plantation in Bali is the "Sari Coffee Plantation" located in the Kintamani area. The plantation is known for its Arabica and Robusta coffee and offers a variety of activities such as coffee tastings, tours of the plantation, and even a traditional Balinese coffee ceremony.

In addition to coffee, Bali is also home to a variety of tea plantations. The most popular of which is the "Jatiluwih Green Land" located in the Tabanan Regency. The plantation is known for its high-quality tea and offers a variety of activities such as tea tastings, tours of the plantation, and even a traditional Balinese tea ceremony.

Another popular tea plantation in Bali is the "Bukit Sari Tea Plantation" located in the Bedugul area. The plantation is known for its high-quality tea and offers a variety of activities such as tea tastings, tours of the plantation, and even a traditional Balinese tea ceremony.

In terms of expenses, visiting a coffee or tea plantation in Bali is relatively affordable. A tour of a coffee or tea plantation typically costs around $5 - $10 USD, and a coffee or tea tasting typically costs around $3 - $5 USD. Visitors can also purchase coffee or tea directly from the plantation at a reasonable price, with a pound of coffee costing around $10 - $15 USD and a pound of tea costing around $5 - $10 USD.

Bali offers a unique and scenic experience for coffee and tea lovers, with a variety of coffee and tea plantations that offer visitors the opportunity to learn about the process of growing, harvesting, and brewing coffee and tea. A visit to a coffee or tea plantation is a great way to learn about the local culture and taste the delicious coffee and tea that Bali has to offer.

CHAPTER 9: SHOPPING AND NIGHTLIFE

Artisanal Crafts And Souvenirs

There are many different types of artisanal crafts and souvenirs that you can purchase in Bali. Some of the most popular include traditional textiles, such as batik and ikat fabrics, hand-carved wooden statues, and stone carvings. You can also find a wide variety of jewelry and accessories, including beaded necklaces, bracelets, and earrings. Additionally, there are many different types of handbags, purses, and other leather goods available.

One of the best places to purchase artisanal crafts and souvenirs in Bali is at the local markets. These markets are found throughout the island and offer a wide variety of items for purchase. Some of the most popular markets include the Ubud Art Market, the Seminyak Square, and the Kuta Art Market.

When shopping for artisanal crafts and souvenirs in Bali, it is important to keep in mind that prices can vary widely. This is due to the fact that many of the items are handmade and the quality can vary. It is also important to keep in mind that bargaining is a common practice in Bali, so don't be afraid to negotiate for a better price.

The cost of artisanal crafts and souvenirs in Bali can vary widely depending on the item and the quality. However, on average, you can expect to pay anywhere from $5 to $50 for most items. For example, a traditional batik sarong can cost around $10 to $20, while a hand-carved wooden statue can cost anywhere from $25 to $50. Handmade jewelry and accessories can also be found for relatively low prices, with most items costing around $5 to $15.

In addition to traditional artisanal crafts and souvenirs, you can also find a wide variety of modern and contemporary items in Bali. These include paintings, photographs, and sculptures created by local artists. These items can be found in galleries and studios throughout the island and can be quite expensive, with prices ranging from $100 to $1000.

Bali is an amazing place to purchase artisanal crafts and souvenirs, and there is something to suit every taste and budget. From traditional batik fabrics and hand-carved wooden statues to contemporary paintings and sculptures, you can find a wide variety of items to take home as a memory of your trip. With the average prices, you can expect to pay anywhere from $5 to $50 for most items, but some of the art piece can be expensive. Remember to bargain for a better price, it's a common practice in Bali.

Local Fashion And Textiles

One of the most popular traditional textiles in Bali is batik. Batik is a method of creating designs on fabric using wax and dye. The process begins by applying wax to the fabric in the desired pattern, and then the fabric is dyed. The wax acts as a resist, preventing the dye from penetrating the covered areas. This process can be repeated multiple times to create complex patterns and designs. Batik is often used to create sarongs, scarves, and shirts, and can be found in markets and shops throughout Bali.

Another traditional textile in Bali is ikat. Ikat is a method of dyeing yarn before it is woven into fabric. The yarn is tied and dyed in the desired pattern, and then woven into fabric. The result is a fabric with a unique, blurred pattern that is similar to batik. Ikat is often used to create traditional clothing, such as the kebaya, a traditional blouse worn by women in Bali.

In addition to traditional textiles, there is also a thriving fashion scene in Bali. The island is home to many local designers who create unique and contemporary clothing and accessories. These designers often use traditional fabrics and techniques, such as batik and ikat, in their creations. This blend of tradition and modernity results in a unique and exciting fashion scene that is well worth exploring.

When shopping for local fashion and textiles in Bali, it is important to keep in mind that prices can vary widely. This is due to the fact that many of the items are handmade and the quality can vary. It is also important to keep in mind that bargaining is a common practice in Bali, so don't be afraid to negotiate for a better price.

The cost of local fashion and textiles in Bali can vary widely depending on the item and the quality. However, on average, you can expect to pay anywhere from $10 to $50 for most items. A traditional batik sarong can cost around $15 to $25, while a ikat fabric can cost around $20 to $30. A modern clothing made by local designer can cost around $30 to $80. Handmade jewelry and accessories can also be found for relatively low prices, with most items costing around $5 to $15.

Another great way to experience local fashion and textiles in Bali is by visiting the many markets and shops on the island. These markets and shops offer a wide variety of items for purchase and are a great way to get a sense of the local fashion and textile scene. Some of the most popular markets and shops include the Ubud Art Market, Seminyak Square, and the Kuta Art Market.

It's also worth noting that Bali is also known for its surf wear fashion, which is the combination of surf culture with the local textile. You can find many brands that offer surf wear clothing and accessories with a touch of Balinese culture. These items tend to be more expensive than traditional textiles, with prices ranging from $50 to $150.

Night Clubs And Bars

The island is home to a wide variety of night clubs and bars, making it a great destination for those looking to party and have a good time. Whether you're looking for a casual beach bar or a high-end nightclub, Bali has something to offer for everyone.

One of the most popular nightlife destinations in Bali is Kuta. This bustling town is known for its lively atmosphere and wide variety of bars and clubs. Some of the most popular bars and clubs in Kuta include Sky Garden, Paddy's, and Bounty. These venues offer a wide variety of music and entertainment, making them a great place to party and dance the night away.

Another popular nightlife destination in Bali is Seminyak. This upscale area is known for its high-end bars and clubs, such as

Potato Head Beach Club and La Favela. These venues offer a more upscale and sophisticated atmosphere, with live music and high-end cocktails.

If you're looking for a more laid-back nightlife experience, you might want to check out the beach bars in Bali. These bars are often located directly on the beach and offer a casual atmosphere with great views of the ocean. Some of the most popular beach bars in Bali include Single Fin, Old Man's, and Beach Club at Finns.

The cost of going to night clubs and bars in Bali can vary widely depending on the venue and the time of the week. On average, you can expect to pay around $10 to $20 for a drink at most bars and clubs. Cover charges for clubs can vary widely, with some venues charging as little as $5 and others charging up to $30. It's also worth noting that some venues in Bali have a dress code, so it's best to check in advance to make sure you're dressed appropriately.

If you're looking to save money on drinks, it's worth noting that many bars and clubs in Bali offer happy hour specials. These specials often feature discounted drinks or free drinks with the purchase of a meal. Additionally, many venues offer package deals, such as all-you-can-drink specials, that can save you money in the long run.

In addition to bars and clubs, there are also many other nightlife options in Bali. These include live music venues, comedy clubs, and cinemas. These venues offer a wide variety of entertainment and are a great way to experience the local culture.

When it comes to nightlife, Bali is a great destination that offers something for everyone. From casual beach bars to high-end nightclubs, there is a wide variety of venues to choose from. The cost of going to night clubs and bars in Bali can vary widely depending on the venue and the time of the week, but on average you can expect to pay around $10 to $20 for a drink and cover charges for clubs can vary widely. Keep in mind that many venues offer happy hour specials and package deals, so it's worth checking in advance to see if there are any deals available.

Another popular nightlife destination in Bali is Canggu. This trendy area has become increasingly popular in recent years, and it offers a wide variety of bars and clubs, such as Old Man's, The Lawn, and Echo Beach Club. These venues offer a more laid-back atmosphere and are a great place to party and enjoy the beautiful beach views.

Ubud, Bali's cultural heart, is also a great place to experience the nightlife. Although it's not known for its clubbing scene, Ubud offers a wide variety of bars and lounges that cater to a more mature crowd. Some of the most popular bars and lounges in Ubud include Indus Restaurant & Bar, Sip Wine Bar, and The Yellow Flower. These venues offer a relaxed atmosphere and are a great place to unwind and enjoy a drink.

It's also worth noting that Bali is known for its night markets, which offer a wide variety of food, drink and shopping. These markets are a great way to experience the local culture and are a great place to grab a bite to eat and enjoy a drink. Some of the most popular night markets in Bali include the Ubud Night Market, the Jimbaran Night Market, and the Kuta Night Market.

To sum up, Bali offers a wide variety of night clubs and bars to fit every taste and budget. From the bustling clubs and bars of Kuta, to the upscale venues of Seminyak, and laid-back beach bars of Canggu, there is something for everyone. Prices can vary widely, with drinks averaging around $10 to $20, and cover charges for clubs ranging from $5 to $30. Keep in mind that many venues offer happy hour specials and package deals, so it's worth checking in advance to see if there are any deals available. Additionally, there are also other nightlife options such as live music venues, comedy clubs, and cinemas, as well as night markets, to explore.

CHAPTER 10: FAMILY-FRIENDLY ACTIVITIES

Adventure Parks And Zoos

One of the most popular adventure parks in Bali is Bali Treetop Adventure Park. This park offers a wide variety of activities for visitors, including ziplining, rope courses, and rock climbing. The park is located in the beautiful Ubud area and offers visitors a chance to enjoy the natural beauty of Bali while also getting a thrill. Prices for entry to the park start at around $20 for adults and $15 for children.

Another popular adventure park in Bali is Bali Safari and Marine Park. This park offers visitors a chance to see a wide variety of wildlife, including lions, tigers, elephants, and many more. The park also offers a wide variety of activities, including a safari ride, animal shows, and an elephant ride. Prices for entry to the park start at around $40 for adults and $30 for children.

For those looking for a more water-based adventure, Bali Wake Park is a great option. This park offers visitors a chance to try their hand at wakeboarding and cable skiing. The park is located in the beautiful Sanur area and offers visitors a chance to enjoy the natural beauty of Bali while also getting a thrill on the water.

Prices for entry to the park start at around $30 for adults and $20 for children.

For families with children, Bali Bird Park is a great option. This park offers visitors a chance to see a wide variety of birds, including parrots, macaws, and many more. The park also offers a wide variety of activities, including bird shows, an aviary, and a playground. Prices for entry to the park start at around $20 for adults and $15 for children.

For those looking for a more educational experience, Bali Butterfly Park is a great option. This park offers visitors a chance to see a wide variety of butterflies, as well as other insects. The park also offers a wide variety of activities, including guided tours, an insect museum, and a playground. Prices for entry to the park start at around $10 for adults and $5 for children.

It's worth noting that many adventure parks and zoos in Bali offer package deals that include multiple activities, such as animal encounters and shows, for an additional cost. These package deals can save you money in the long run and provide a more comprehensive experience.

Children's Museums And Activities

One of the many unique offerings on the island is the variety of children's museums and activities available. These museums and activities provide a fun and educational experience for children of all ages, while also giving parents and caregivers the opportunity to relax and enjoy the island.

One of the most popular children's museums in Bali is the Bali Treetop Adventure Park. This park features a variety of aerial and ground-based activities, including zip lining, rope courses, and obstacle courses. The park also features a children's playground and picnic areas, making it the perfect destination for families. The park is located in the Ubud area and admission is around $20 for adult and $15 for children.

Another popular children's activity in Bali is the Bali Safari and Marine Park. This park features a variety of animal exhibits and shows, including elephants, tigers, lions, and more. The park also features a children's playground and picnic areas, making it the perfect destination for families. Admission is around $40 for adult and $30 for children.

For children who are interested in science and technology, the Museum Teknologi is a must-see destination. This museum features a variety of interactive exhibits and activities, including a planetarium and a science lab. The museum is located in the Denpasar area and admission is around $5 for adult and $3 for children.

If your child is into art and culture, the Museum Puri Lukisan is a great option. This museum features a variety of traditional Balinese art, including paintings, sculptures, and carvings. The museum is located in the Ubud area and admission is around $5 for adult and $3 for children.

For a fun and unique experience, the Bali Butterfly Park is a great option. This park features a variety of live butterflies and other insects, as well as a children's playground and picnic areas. The park is located in the Tabanan area and admission is around $10 for adult and $7 for children.

In addition to the museums and activities listed above, Bali also offers a variety of other children's activities such as water park, theme park, and many more. These activities provide a fun and educational experience for children of all ages, while also giving parents and caregivers the opportunity to relax and enjoy the island.

When it comes to expenses, Bali is relatively affordable compared to other tourist destinations. Accommodations and food are relatively inexpensive, and many of the activities listed above are also reasonably priced. However, it's always best to do some research ahead of time and make a budget for your trip to ensure that you are able to make the most of your time in Bali without breaking the bank

Wildlife Safari And Ecotourism

One of the many unique offerings on the island is the variety of wildlife safari and ecotourism activities available. These activities provide a chance to explore the natural beauty of Bali and learn about the island's diverse array of flora and fauna.

One of the most popular ecotourism activities in Bali is the Bali Safari and Marine Park. This park features a variety of animal exhibits and shows, including elephants, tigers, lions, and more. The park also offers a variety of safari options, including a night safari and a jungle hopper safari, which allows visitors to explore the park on foot or by boat. The park is located in the Gianyar area, admission is around $40 for adult and $30 for children.

Another popular wildlife safari activity in Bali is the Bali Bird Park. This park is home to over 1000 birds from 250 different species, including endangered species such as the Bali Starling and the Javan Hawk-Eagle. The park also features a variety of interactive exhibits and activities, including a bird show and a bird feeding area. The park is located in the Singapadu area and admission is around $20 for adult and $15 for children.

For a more immersive ecotourism experience, the Bali Tamblingan Trekking is a great option. This trek takes visitors through the Tamblingan Forest, a protected area of tropical rainforest home to a diverse array of flora and fauna. The trek is led by experienced guides who provide information about the forest and its inhabitants along the way. The trek is located in the Buleleng area and the cost is around $50 per person.

For those interested in marine wildlife, the Bali Marine Walk is a unique experience. This activity takes visitors on a guided walk through an underwater tunnel, where they can see a variety of marine life, including sharks, rays, and tropical fish. The walk is located in the Tanjung Benoa area and the cost is around $25 per person.

If you are looking for an adventure, the Bali Elephant Ride and Safari is a great option. This activity allows visitors to ride on the back of an elephant through the jungle, while learning about the elephant's behavior and habitat. The ride is located in the Gianyar area and the cost is around $70 per person.

In addition to the activities listed above, Bali also offers a variety of other ecotourism activities such as snorkeling, diving, and bird watching. These activities provide a chance to explore the natural beauty of Bali and learn about the island's diverse array of flora and fauna.

When it comes to expenses, Bali is relatively affordable compared to other ecotourism destinations. Accommodations and food are relatively inexpensive, and many of the activities listed above are also reasonably priced. However, it's always best to do some research ahead of time and make a budget for your trip to ensure that you are able to make the most of your time in Bali without breaking the bank.

Bali offers a wide variety of wildlife safari and ecotourism activities that provide a chance to explore the natural beauty of the island and learn about its diverse array of flora and fauna. These activities range from visiting wildlife parks, trekking in protected rainforest, marine walk, elephant ride and safari, and many more. Bali is also relatively affordable compared to other ecotourism destinations, and making a budget for your trip can help you enjoy your trip without breaking the bank.

CHAPTER 11: ITINERARY SUGGESTIONS

A week in Bali

A week in Bali can be a magical experience, filled with stunning beaches, delicious food, and rich culture. The island is located in Indonesia and is known for its tropical climate, beautiful landscapes, and friendly locals.

The cost of a week-long trip to Bali will depend on a variety of factors, such as the time of year you visit, your accommodation choice, and your travel style. On average, a budget-friendly trip to Bali can cost around $500-$700 USD per person for a week, including flights, accommodation, transportation, and food. However, if you opt for more luxurious options, the cost can easily double or triple.

One of the biggest expenses for a trip to Bali will be the flight. Flights from major cities in the US to Bali can cost anywhere from $600-$1000 USD depending on the time of year and the airline you choose. Once you arrive in Bali, you can expect to spend around $15-$20 USD per day on transportation, which includes local buses, taxis, and motorbike rentals.

Accommodation in Bali can range from budget-friendly hostels to luxurious resorts. A budget-friendly option would be staying in a homestay or hostel, which can cost around $10-$15 USD per night. For a more comfortable option, you can expect to pay around $30-$50 USD per night for a mid-range hotel or guesthouse. If you're looking for a more luxurious option, you can expect to pay around $100-$300 USD per night for a high-end resort or villa.

Food in Bali is delicious and relatively cheap. A meal at a local warung (Indonesian restaurant) can cost around $2-$5 USD. A meal at a more upscale restaurant can cost around $10-$20 USD. If you're on a budget, you can save money by cooking your own meals or eating street food.

A week in Bali can be a magical and affordable experience. With beautiful beaches, delicious food, and rich culture, Bali is a destination that should be on everyone's travel bucket list. With careful planning and budgeting, you can enjoy all that Bali has to offer without breaking the bank.

10 Days In Bali

A 10-day trip to Bali can be a truly unforgettable experience, with its stunning beaches, delicious food, and rich culture. The island is located in Indonesia and is known for its tropical climate, beautiful landscapes, and friendly locals.

The cost of a 10-day trip to Bali will depend on a variety of factors, such as the time of year you visit, your accommodation choice, and your travel style. On average, a budget-friendly trip to Bali can cost around $800-$1200 USD per person for 10 days, including flights, accommodation, transportation, and food. However, if you opt for more luxurious options, the cost can easily double or triple.

One of the biggest expenses for a trip to Bali will be the flight. Flights from major cities in the US to Bali can cost anywhere from $600-$1000 USD depending on the time of year and the airline you choose. Once you arrive in Bali, you can expect to spend around $15-$20 USD per day on transportation, which includes local buses, taxis, and motorbike rentals.

Accommodation in Bali can range from budget-friendly hostels to luxurious resorts. A budget-friendly option would be staying in a homestay or hostel, which can cost around $10-$15 USD per night. For a more comfortable option, you can expect to pay around $30-$50 USD per night for a mid-range hotel or guesthouse. If you're looking for a more luxurious option, you can expect to pay around $100-$300 USD per night for a high-end resort or villa.

Food in Bali is delicious and relatively cheap. A meal at a local warung (Indonesian restaurant) can cost around $2-$5 USD. A meal at a more upscale restaurant can cost around $10-$20 USD. If you're on a budget, you can save money by cooking your own meals or eating street food.

When it comes to activities, there are plenty of things to do in Bali. Some popular activities include:

Surfing: Bali is known for its great surf spots, and there are plenty of surf schools where you can learn how to catch a wave. Prices vary, but you can expect to pay around $40-$60 USD for a 2-hour lesson.

Yoga: Bali is a popular destination for yoga enthusiasts, and there are plenty of studios and retreats where you can practice. Prices vary, but you can expect to pay around $10-$20 USD for a single class.

Temples: Bali is home to some beautiful temples that are worth visiting. Most temples are free to enter, but some require a small donation.

Beaches: Bali is home to some of the most beautiful beaches in the world. Some popular beaches include Kuta, Seminyak, and Nusa Dua. Most beaches are free to enter, but some may require a small fee for parking or umbrella rental.

Shopping: Bali is a great place to shop for souvenirs and local crafts. Some popular shopping areas include Ubud and Seminyak.

Trekking and Hiking: Bali is home to some beautiful trekking and hiking trails that offer great views of the island's landscape. Popular trails include Mount Batur, Mount Agung, and the rice terraces in Ubud.

Spa and Massages: Bali is known for its spa and massage treatments that are offered at a reasonable price. A traditional Balinese massage can cost around $10-$15 USD for an hour.

Water Sports: Bali offers a wide range of water sports such as snorkeling, scuba diving, and parasailing. Prices vary depending on the activity and location, but you can expect to pay around $30-$50 USD for a snorkeling or diving trip and around $50-$100 USD for a parasailing excursion.

Cultural tours: Bali is rich in culture and tradition, and there are many tours available that will take you to visit traditional villages, temples, and other cultural sites. Prices vary, but you can expect to pay around $20-$50 USD for a half-day tour.

Culinary tours: Bali is also known for its delicious food, and there are many culinary tours available that will take you to visit local markets and traditional warungs (Indonesian restaurants). Prices vary, but you can expect to pay around $30-$50 USD for a half-day tour.

In addition to the above expenses, it is also recommended to budget for tips, souvenirs, and unexpected expenses. It's also important to note that some activities and tours may require additional fees or entrance fees.

A 10-day trip to Bali can be a truly unforgettable experience, with its stunning beaches, delicious food, and rich culture. With careful planning and budgeting, you can enjoy all that Bali has to offer without breaking the bank. However, it's important to keep in mind that the prices mentioned here are just an estimate and may fluctuate depending on the time of year and your specific travel plans.

Two Weeks In Bali

Two weeks in Bali can be a truly immersive experience, allowing you to fully immerse yourself in the island's stunning beaches, delicious food, and rich culture. Bali is located in Indonesia and is known for its tropical climate, beautiful landscapes, and friendly locals.

The cost of a two-week trip to Bali will depend on a variety of factors, such as the time of year you visit, your accommodation choice, and your travel style. On average, a budget-friendly trip to Bali can cost around $1000-$1500 USD per person for two weeks, including flights, accommodation, transportation, and food. However, if you opt for more luxurious options, the cost can easily double or triple.

One of the biggest expenses for a trip to Bali will be the flight. Flights from major cities in the US to Bali can cost anywhere from $600-$1000 USD depending on the time of year and the airline you choose. Once you arrive in Bali, you can expect to spend around $15-$20 USD per day on transportation, which includes local buses, taxis, and motorbike rentals.

Accommodation in Bali can range from budget-friendly hostels to luxurious resorts. A budget-friendly option would be staying in a homestay or hostel, which can cost around $10-$15 USD per night. For a more comfortable option, you can expect to pay around $30-$50 USD per night for a mid-range hotel or guesthouse. If you're looking for a more luxurious option, you can expect to pay around $100-$300 USD per night for a high-end resort or villa.

Food in Bali is delicious and relatively cheap. A meal at a local warung (Indonesian restaurant) can cost around $2-$5 USD. A meal at a more upscale restaurant can cost around $10-$20 USD. If you're on a budget, you can save money by cooking your own meals or eating street food.

Off-the-beaten-path destinations

However, with so many tourists flocking to the island, it can be difficult to find a truly authentic experience. Fortunately, there are still many off-the-beaten-path destinations in Bali that offer a more authentic and less crowded experience.

One of the best off-the-beaten-path destinations in Bali is the village of Munduk. Located in the mountains of central Bali, Munduk offers a peaceful and secluded experience with stunning views of rice terraces, waterfalls, and lush jungle. Munduk is also home to a number of traditional villages and temples that offer a glimpse into the island's rich culture and history. Accommodation in Munduk can range from budget-friendly homestays to luxurious villas, with prices averaging around $20-$50 USD per night.

Another great off-the-beaten-path destination in Bali is the town of Amed. Located on the northeastern coast of the island, Amed is known for its traditional fishing villages, secluded beaches, and world-class diving and snorkeling. Amed is also home to a number of traditional salt farms and coral reefs that offer a unique and authentic experience. Accommodation in Amed can range from budget-friendly homestays to luxurious resorts, with prices averaging around $30-$50 USD per night.

For those interested in exploring Bali's rich cultural heritage, the village of Tenganan is a must-visit destination. This ancient village is known for its traditional architecture, intricate woven fabrics, and unique customs and rituals. Tenganan is also home to a number of traditional temples and shrines that offer a glimpse into the island's rich spiritual history. Accommodation in Tenganan is limited, but there are a few homestays and guesthouses available, with prices averaging around $15-$20 USD per night.

For those looking for a more adventurous experience, the island of Nusa Penida is a great off-the-beaten-path destination. This small island located just off the coast of Bali is known for its rugged landscapes, stunning cliffs, and hidden beaches. Nusa Penida is also home to a number of world-class diving and snorkeling sites, as well as a number of traditional villages and temples. Accommodation in Nusa Penida can range from budget-friendly homestays to luxurious resorts, with prices averaging around $30-$50 USD per night.

Off-the-beaten-path destinations in Bali offer a more authentic and secluded experience than the more popular tourist areas. These destinations are also relatively affordable, with accommodation and transportation costs averaging around $20-$50 USD per night. However, it's important to keep in mind that prices can vary depending on the time of year and your specific travel plans.

CHAPTER 12: SAFETY AND PRACTICAL INFORMATION

Safety Precautions

It is important to take safety precautions to ensure a safe and enjoyable trip.

One of the most important safety precautions to take when traveling to Bali is to make sure that you have comprehensive travel insurance. This will cover any medical expenses in the event of an accident or illness, as well as cover any lost or stolen belongings. The cost of travel insurance can vary depending on the provider and the level of coverage, but it is typically a small price to pay for the peace of mind that it provides.

Another important safety precaution is to be aware of the local laws and customs. Bali is a predominantly Hindu island, and it is important to be respectful of the local culture and traditions. This includes covering up when visiting temples, not touching or pointing at religious artifacts, and not engaging in activities that may be considered disrespectful, such as public displays of affection.

When it comes to personal safety, it is important to be aware of your surroundings at all times. This includes being cautious of pickpockets and scam artists, especially in tourist areas. It is also a good idea to avoid carrying large amounts of cash, and to keep your valuables in a safe place.

When it comes to transportation, it is important to be aware of the risks of motorcycle accidents. Many tourists choose to rent motorcycles or scooters to get around, but it is important to be aware of the risks and to take precautions such as wearing a helmet. Additionally, it is important to be aware of the traffic laws and to drive defensively.

When it comes to expenses, Bali is generally considered to be a budget-friendly destination. Accommodation and food are relatively inexpensive, and there are plenty of affordable activities to enjoy, such as hiking, surfing, and exploring the local temples. However, it is important to be aware of hidden costs, such as taxes and service charges, which can add up.

Bali is a beautiful and vibrant destination that offers something for everyone. By taking a few safety precautions and being aware of the local laws and customs, you can ensure a safe and enjoyable trip. While expenses can be kept low, always be aware of hidden costs and make sure to have comprehensive travel insurance to keep you safe and secure.

Currency And Money

Currency and money are an important aspect of any travel destination, and Bali is no exception. The official currency of Bali and Indonesia is the Indonesian Rupiah (IDR). It is important to be familiar with the currency and the exchange rate before traveling to Bali, as it can be difficult to find places that accept foreign currency.

The most common denomination of the IDR is the 100,000, 50,000, 20,000 and 10,000 note. It's important to note that you will probably receive a lot of smaller denominations while exchanging currency or receiving change, as larger notes are often hard to come by. It's also important to keep in mind that many places do not accept IDR notes with any kind of damage, so make sure to check the notes you receive before you leave the exchange office.

It is a good idea to have a mix of cash and credit cards when traveling to Bali. Many small businesses, such as street vendors and local restaurants, only accept cash, while more upscale businesses and hotels may accept credit cards. It's also a good idea to have a bit of cash on hand for unexpected expenses, such as transportation and tips.

When it comes to exchanging currency, it is important to be aware of the exchange rate and to shop around for the best deal. Currency exchange offices are widely available in Bali, and can be found at the airport, major hotels, and in tourist areas. However, it is important to be aware that not all currency exchange offices offer the same rate, and it is a good idea to compare rates before exchanging currency.

ATMs are widely available in Bali, and can be found in most tourist areas and major towns. However, it is important to be aware that some ATMs may charge a fee for withdrawals, and that there may be a limit on the amount of cash that can be withdrawn. it's also a good idea to inform your bank and credit card company that you will be traveling to Bali, to avoid any issues with blocked transactions.

When it comes to shopping and expenses in Bali, it is important to be aware of the prices and to negotiate when appropriate. Many street vendors and local shops will be willing to negotiate on price, and it is a good idea to be familiar with the local prices to ensure that you are not overpaying. Additionally, it's important to be aware of the taxes and service charges that may be added to the final bill, which can add up quickly.

Currency and money are an important aspect of traveling to Bali. It is important to be familiar with the currency and the exchange rate, and to have a mix of cash and credit cards. Currency exchange offices and ATMs are widely available, but it is important to be aware of the fees and limits associated with them. When shopping and expenses in Bali, it is important to be aware of the prices and to negotiate when appropriate. Being aware of these factors can help ensure that you have a safe and enjoyable trip to Bali.

Communication And Internet Access

Communication and internet access are essential for any traveler, and Bali is no exception. With the increasing reliance on technology in today's world, it is important to be aware of the communication and internet options available in Bali.

When it comes to phone service, it is important to be aware that Bali is part of Indonesia and has a different area code than the rest of the country. The country code for Indonesia is +62 and to call a local number in Bali you will need to dial the area code (0361) before the local number. It's also important to be aware that roaming charges can be quite high, so it is a good idea to check with your service provider before traveling to Bali.

An alternative option is to purchase a local SIM card with a prepaid plan. These can be easily purchased at the airport or at most phone shops in Bali. You will need to provide a passport or ID as proof of identification and the SIM card can be activated on the spot. This can save you a lot of money on roaming charges, and also give you a local number to make and receive calls while in Bali.

When it comes to internet access, Bali has a good infrastructure and you can find WiFi in most hotels, restaurants and cafes. However, the speed and reliability of the internet can vary depending on the location. If you need to rely on internet access for work or other important matters, it's a good idea to bring a portable hotspot or a Mi-Fi device, which can provide more reliable internet access.

There are also many internet cafes in Bali, which can be a good option for travelers who do not have their own devices. These cafes typically offer high-speed internet access, as well as computers and printers for a small fee.

Another important aspect of communication in Bali is being aware of the language barrier. While many people in Bali speak English, it is not widely spoken and it can be difficult to communicate with locals in some areas. A phrasebook or translation app can be helpful for communicating with locals and navigating unfamiliar areas.

Communication and internet access are essential for any traveler, and Bali is no exception. Phone service can be expensive, but purchasing a local SIM card with a prepaid plan can save you a lot of money on roaming charges. Internet access is widely available in Bali, but the speed and reliability can vary depending on the location. It's a good idea to bring a portable hotspot or a Mi-Fi device to ensure reliable internet access. Being aware of the language barrier can also help to navigate unfamiliar areas. Being aware of these factors can help ensure that you have a safe and enjoyable trip to Bali.

Health And Medical Care

Health and medical care are important considerations for any traveler, and Bali is no exception. While Bali is generally considered to be a safe destination, it is important to be aware of the potential health risks and to take appropriate precautions.

One of the most important things to be aware of when traveling to Bali is the risk of dengue fever. Dengue fever is a viral illness transmitted by mosquitoes, and it is present in Bali year-round. To protect yourself from dengue fever, it is important to take precautions such as wearing long-sleeved clothing and using mosquito repellent. Additionally, it is a good idea to avoid standing water, which is a breeding ground for mosquitoes.

Another important consideration is food and water safety. Bali is known for its delicious street food, but it is important to be aware of the risks of food poisoning. It is a good idea to stick to well-established restaurants and street vendors, and to avoid eating raw or undercooked food. Additionally, it is important to be aware of the risks of water-borne illnesses and to stick to bottled water for drinking and brushing teeth.

When it comes to medical care in Bali, it is important to be aware that the level of care can vary depending on the location. Many major tourist areas have well-equipped hospitals and clinics, but the quality of care can be lower in more remote areas. It is a good idea to have comprehensive travel insurance, which will cover any medical expenses in the event of an accident or illness.

Additionally, it's important to have a copy of your insurance policy and contact information with you.

It's also a good idea to research the location of the nearest hospital or clinic in the area where you are staying, in case of an emergency. Some hospitals in Bali have a good reputation, such as Sanglah General Hospital in Denpasar or BIMC Hospital in Kuta. It's important to have a reliable way of communicating, such as a local SIM card, in case you need to call for help.

It's also a good idea to bring any necessary medications with you, as well as a basic first-aid kit. This can include things such as pain relievers, anti-diarrhea medication, and any prescription medications you may need.

Health and medical care are important considerations for any traveler, and Bali is no exception. Dengue fever and food and water-borne illnesses are potential health risks, and it is important to take appropriate precautions. Medical care in Bali can vary depending on the location, and it is important to have comprehensive travel insurance and to research the location of the nearest hospital or clinic. It's also a good idea to bring any necessary medications with you, as well as a basic first-aid kit.

Being aware of these factors can help ensure that you have a safe and enjoyable trip to Bali.

Tips For Travelers

Be aware of the local customs and laws. Bali is a predominantly Hindu island, and it is important to be respectful of the local culture and traditions. This includes covering up when visiting temples, not touching or pointing at religious artifacts, and not engaging in activities that may be considered disrespectful, such as public displays of affection.

Take appropriate precautions against dengue fever. Dengue fever is a viral illness transmitted by mosquitoes, and it is present in Bali year-round. To protect yourself from dengue fever, it is important to take precautions such as wearing long-sleeved clothing and using mosquito repellent. Additionally, it is a good idea to avoid standing water, which is a breeding ground for mosquitoes.

Be aware of the risks of food and water-borne illnesses. Bali is known for its delicious street food, but it is important to be aware of the risks of food poisoning. It is a good idea to stick to well-established restaurants and street vendors, and to avoid eating raw or undercooked food. Additionally, it is important to be aware of the risks of water-borne illnesses and to stick to bottled water for drinking and brushing teeth.

Have comprehensive travel insurance. Medical care in Bali can vary depending on the location, and it is important to have comprehensive travel insurance to cover any medical expenses in the event of an accident or illness. Additionally, it's important to have a copy of your insurance policy and contact information with you.

Research the location of the nearest hospital or clinic in the area where you are staying, in case of an emergency. Some hospitals in Bali have a good reputation, such as Sanglah General Hospital in Denpasar or BIMC Hospital in Kuta. It's important to have a reliable way of communicating, such as a local SIM card, in case you need to call for help.

Have a mix of cash and credit cards. Many small businesses, such as street vendors and local restaurants, only accept cash, while more upscale businesses and hotels may accept credit cards. It's also a good idea to have a bit of cash on hand for unexpected expenses, such as transportation and tips.

Be aware of the language barrier. While many people in Bali speak English, it is not widely spoken and it can be difficult to communicate with locals in some areas. A phrasebook or translation app can be helpful for communicating with locals and navigating unfamiliar areas.

Be prepared for the weather. Bali has a tropical climate and it can be hot and humid, so it is important to stay hydrated and to wear lightweight clothing. Additionally, it is a good idea to bring sunscreen and a hat to protect yourself from the sun.

Be mindful of your surroundings and be aware of pickpocketing and scam artists, especially in tourist areas.

Finally, don't forget to relax and enjoy your time in Bali! Take in the beautiful scenery, try the delicious food, and immerse yourself in the culture.

Tips For Traveling With Pets

Traveling with pets can be a rewarding experience, but it is important to be aware of the specific considerations and regulations when planning to bring your furry companion to Bali. Here are some tips for traveling with pets to Bali:

Research the regulations and requirements for pet travel to Bali. Each country has its own set of rules and regulations regarding pet travel, and it is important to be aware of these before planning your trip. This may include specific documentation and vaccinations required, as well as quarantine regulations. It's also important to check with the airline and find out their specific regulations.

Consult with a veterinarian. Before traveling with your pet, it's important to consult with a veterinarian to make sure your pet is healthy and up-to-date on all necessary vaccinations. Your vet can also help you to determine if your pet is fit to travel and can provide a health certificate if required.

Make sure your pet is microchipped. Microchipping is a permanent identification method that can be used to locate your pet if they get lost. This can be especially important if you are traveling to a foreign country.

Invest in a sturdy, comfortable carrier for your pet. Your pet will be traveling in a carrier for a significant amount of time, so it's important to make sure that the carrier is comfortable, secure, and well-ventilated.

Pack a travel kit for your pet. This can include items such as food and water dishes, a leash and collar, toys, and any medications your pet may need.

Plan your accommodation in advance. Not all hotels or vacation rentals allow pets, so it's important to research your options and make a reservation in advance. Consider also if they have any special requirements or fees for pets.

Be aware of the local weather and climate. Bali has a tropical climate and it can be hot and humid, so it is important to make sure that your pet is comfortable and has access to plenty of water. Make sure you have the contact information for a local veterinarian in case of an emergency.

Be aware of the local laws and regulations regarding pets. Some areas may have specific regulations regarding pets, such as leash laws or designated areas where pets are allowed.

Finally, it's important to consider your pet's emotional well-being when traveling. Some pets may not be comfortable with travel, so it's important to make sure that your pet is happy and relaxed throughout the journey.

LGBTQ+ Travel Information

Be aware of the local laws and attitudes towards LGBTQ+ individuals. Indonesia as a country has laws that criminalize homosexuality and same-sex sexual activity. While these laws are not always enforced, it is important to be aware of the potential risks and to exercise caution, especially in more conservative areas. Discrimination and harassment based on sexual orientation and gender identity can also occur, and it is important to be aware of this and to be prepared to deal with it if it arises.

Research accommodations that are LGBTQ+ friendly. While most hotels and vacation rentals in Bali are welcoming to all guests, it is important to research accommodations that are specifically LGBTQ+ friendly. These accommodations may have policies in place to ensure that all guests feel safe and comfortable.

Be discreet in public spaces. While Bali is a relatively liberal destination, it is important to be discreet in public spaces, especially in more conservative areas. This may include avoiding public displays of affection and being mindful of how you dress and present yourself.

Find LGBTQ+ friendly nightlife and events. Bali has a vibrant nightlife scene, and it is important to find LGBTQ+ friendly venues and events. These venues may be more accepting and welcoming to LGBTQ+ individuals, and can be a great way to meet other like-minded travelers.

Be prepared for language barriers. While many people in Bali speak English, it is not widely spoken, and it can be difficult to communicate with locals in some areas. A translation app can be helpful for communicating with locals and navigating unfamiliar areas.

Consider traveling with a tour company that caters to the LGBTQ+ community. There are a number of tour companies that cater specifically to the LGBTQ+ community, and these can be a great way to ensure a safe and comfortable trip.

Be aware of the local healthcare options. In case of an emergency, it is important to be aware of the local healthcare options and to have the contact information for a local healthcare provider.

Be aware of your rights as an LGBTQ+ individual. It's important to be aware of your rights as an LGBTQ+ individual, and to have the contact information for local LGBTQ+ organizations in case of an emergency.

Bali is a beautiful and vibrant destination that offers something for everyone, including LGBTQ+ travelers. However, as a destination with a conservative cultural background, it is important for LGBTQ+ travelers to be aware of the specific considerations and regulations when planning their trip. Researching accommodations that are LGBTQ+ friendly, being discreet in public spaces, and finding LGBTQ+ friendly nightlife and events are essential steps in ensuring a safe and comfortable trip.

Being aware of the local laws, healthcare options and rights as an LGBTQ+ individual are also important considerations. Being aware of these factors can help ensure that LGBTQ+ travelers have a safe and enjoyable trip to Bali.

Natural Disasters And Severe Weather

Here are some tips for travelers to Bali to prepare and stay safe during these events:

Be aware of the potential natural disasters and severe weather. Bali is located in a tropical climate and is subject to various natural disasters such as floods, earthquakes, and volcanic eruptions. Additionally, Bali is also prone to severe weather including tropical storms and typhoons. It's important to be aware of the potential risks and to stay informed about the weather and natural disaster warnings.

Research the location of the nearest evacuation centers and emergency shelters. In case of natural disasters and severe weather, it's important to know the location of the nearest evacuation centers and emergency shelters. Make sure to have the contact information for emergency services, and know the emergency plan for your accommodation.

Pack emergency supplies. It's always a good idea to pack a basic emergency kit, including items such as first aid supplies, a flashlight, and extra batteries. It's also a good idea to have a portable power bank to charge your phone, and a backup of important documents, like your passport and insurance policy.

Have a plan in case of evacuation. It's important to have a plan in case of evacuation, which includes knowing the location of the nearest evacuation centers and emergency shelters, and having a way to communicate with loved ones.

Be prepared for power and water outages. Natural disasters and severe weather can cause power and water outages, so it's important to be prepared for this possibility. This may include having a backup source of power, such as a portable power bank, and stocking up on water and non-perishable food.

Avoid low-lying areas and flood-prone areas during floods and heavy rain. Floods and heavy rain can cause flash floods and landslides, it's important to avoid low-lying areas and flood-prone areas during these events.

Follow the instructions of local authorities. In case of natural disasters and severe weather, it's important to follow the instructions of local authorities, including evacuation orders and emergency alerts.

Be aware of the local laws and customs. Natural disasters and severe weather can cause stress and anxiety, and it's important to be aware of the local laws and customs to avoid any misunderstandings.

Emergency services

it is important to be aware of the emergency services that are available in case of an emergency. Here are some tips for travelers to Bali to prepare and stay safe in case of an emergency situation:

Know the emergency contact numbers. It's important to have the emergency contact numbers for the local authorities, such as the police, fire department, and ambulance service. These numbers are usually 110 for the police, 113 for ambulance and 118 for fire department. It's also a good idea to have the contact information for your embassy or consulate, as well as your travel insurance provider.

Have a plan in case of emergency. It's important to have a plan in case of emergency, which includes knowing the location of the nearest emergency services, such as hospitals and clinics, and having a way to communicate with loved ones.

Be aware of the local laws and customs. In case of emergency, it's important to be aware of the local laws and customs to avoid any misunderstandings. This may include knowing the local emergency protocol, such as evacuation procedures and emergency alerts.

Understand the medical facilities and emergency care availability. Bali has a range of medical facilities that vary in terms of quality and availability. Some of the most reputable hospitals include Sanglah General Hospital in Denpasar and BIMC Hospital in Kuta. However, it's important to research the location of the nearest hospital or clinic in the area where you are staying, in case of an emergency.

Get a comprehensive travel insurance. Having comprehensive travel insurance will cover any medical expenses in the event of an accident or illness. It's important to have a copy of your insurance policy and contact information with you, as well as your passport and other important documents.

Be aware of the emergency evacuation procedures. In case of natural disasters or severe weather, it's important to be aware of the emergency evacuation procedures, including the location of the nearest evacuation centers and emergency shelters.

Learn basic first-aid. Knowing basic first-aid can help you in case of an emergency. It's a good idea to bring a first-aid kit with you, and to be familiar with the contents of the kit.

Follow the instructions of local authorities. In case of emergency, it's important to follow the instructions of local authorities, including evacuation orders and emergency alerts.

CONCLUSION

Final Thoughts On Bali

The island has been a popular destination for tourists for decades, and it continues to draw in visitors from all over the world.

One of the main reasons people visit Bali is for its beautiful beaches. Bali's coastline stretches for more than 120 km and is dotted with white sandy beaches, crystal clear waters, and a variety of beach activities. Some of the most popular beaches on the island include Kuta, Seminyak, and Nusa Dua. These beaches offer a variety of options for visitors, from water sports such as surfing and snorkeling, to relaxing on the beach and soaking up the sun.

Another major draw for tourists is Bali's culture and spiritual significance. The island is home to a number of Hindu temples and ceremonies, which offer visitors a glimpse into the island's rich cultural heritage. Visitors can witness traditional dances, ceremonies, and festivals throughout the year, which are a great way to experience the island's culture firsthand. Additionally, many visitors choose to take part in yoga and meditation classes, which are widely available on the island and are a great way to relax and reconnect with nature.

Bali is also known for its vibrant nightlife, with a variety of bars, clubs, and restaurants catering to tourists and locals alike. The island's main tourist areas, such as Kuta and Seminyak, offer a wide range of nightlife options, from lively clubs and bars to more relaxed rooftop bars and lounge areas. Visitors can also enjoy traditional music and dance performances, which take place in a number of venues throughout the island.

Another major aspect of the Bali Experience is its Food and Cuisine. Balinese food is a reflection of the island's rich cultural heritage and its diverse population. The cuisine is a blend of traditional and modern flavors, with a strong emphasis on fresh ingredients, and local spices. Visitors can find a wide range of traditional Balinese dishes, such as nasi goreng (fried rice), sate lilit (minced fish or meat skewers), and lawar (mixed vegetable salad), as well as international cuisine in the island.

The island's natural beauty is another major draw for tourists. Bali is home to a number of beautiful natural landscapes, including lush rice terraces, rugged volcanic landscapes, and dense tropical forests. Visitors can explore these landscapes by hiking, cycling, or taking a guided tour. Some popular natural attractions on the island include the Ubud Rice Terraces, Mount Batur, and the Tegallalang Rice Terraces.

In recent years, Bali has also become known as a destination for wellness and rejuvenation. The island offers a wide range of wellness retreats and spas, which offer visitors the opportunity to relax, rejuvenate, and improve their overall well-being. Visitors can choose from a variety of treatments, such as yoga, massage, and traditional healing therapies, to help them relax and refresh.

Additional Resources For Planning a Trip To Bali

Tourism websites: The official website of the Indonesian Ministry of Tourism (www.indonesia.travel) and the Bali Tourism Board (www.balitourismboard.org) are great sources of information on the island. They provide detailed information on things to see and do, accommodations, transportation, and more.

Travel guides: There are a number of travel guides available that can help you plan your trip to Bali. Some popular options include Lonely Planet Bali & Lombok, Frommer's Bali, and Fodor's Bali. These guides provide detailed information on the island's top attractions, as well as practical tips for getting around and where to eat and stay.

Blogs: There are many travel bloggers who have written about their experiences in Bali. They provide valuable insights, tips, and recommendations on things to do, see and places to stay. They also share their experiences of traveling in Bali, which can help you get an idea of what to expect during your trip.

Social media: Social media platforms such as Instagram, Facebook, and Twitter are great resources for finding out about the latest happenings in Bali. You can follow popular accounts that focus on Bali travel, such as @baligasm or @thebalibible to get inspiration and updates on what's happening on the island.

Online forums: Online travel forums such as TripAdvisor and Lonely Planet's Thorntree are great places to ask questions and get advice from other travelers who have been to Bali. You can also read reviews of hotels, restaurants, and attractions to get an idea of what to expect during your trip.

Online booking platforms: There are a number of online booking platforms, such as Booking.com, Agoda, and Expedia, that can help you find the best deals on accommodations and transportation in Bali. You can compare prices and read reviews to find the best options for your budget and preferences.

In addition to these resources, it is also important to check the latest travel advisories and visa requirements before planning your trip to Bali. The Indonesian Embassy website or the U.S. Department of State website are good sources of information on this topic.

Planning a trip to Bali can be a lot of fun, but it's important to do your research and have access to reliable resources. By taking the time to plan your trip in advance, you can ensure that your experience in Bali is as enjoyable and stress-free as possible.

Made in the USA
Las Vegas, NV
09 August 2023

75869775R00095